AF521604
FORGED
TDE Looped

SECRETS OF THE
Saltwater Fly

SECRETS OF THE Saltwater Fly

Tips and Tales from the World's Great Anglers

f-stop Fitzgerald

Introduction by Lou Tabory
Text by Kenneth Wapner

A Bulfinch Press Book

LITTLE, BROWN AND COMPANY
BOSTON NEW YORK TORONTO LONDON

A Balliett & Fitzgerald Book

First Edition

Produced by Balliett & Fitzgerald, Inc.
Design and map illustrations by Susan Canavan
Text by Kenneth Wapner
Lighting director: Richard McCaffrey
Stylist: Marsha Barrs

ISBN 0-8212-2308-9

Library of Congress Catalog Card Number 96-86105

Front jacket photo: D. L. Mylar Minnow by D. L. Goddard
Back jacket photo: Robert Spaight
Endpapers photo: Detail of tying cabinet
Title page photo: Grey Shrimp by Jens Staal
Page 8 photo: Trio of Lou Tabory designs
Page 109 photo: Pic's Pogy by Tom Piccolo

Individuals interested in original photographs from this book should write to:
f-stop Fitzgerald, 88 James Street, Rosendale, NY 12472

Bulfinch Press is an imprint and trademark of Little, Brown and Company (Inc.)
Published simultaneously in Canada by Little, Brown & Company (Canada) Limited

PRINTED IN CHINA

To my children, Genni and Weston,
may they always enjoy the wonder of
the wind, the waves, and the water.

fsf

Fish die belly-upward and ride to the surface;
it is their way of falling.

André Gide

Contents

Introduction

by Lou Tabory

Perhaps it's the size of the fish, or their wildness, that makes an angler want to fly fish in salt water. Or maybe it's the setting—a rocky, wave-battered coastline; a beautiful, clearwater flat—but there's something that draws people to the sea. It is a humbling domain for an angler, an environment that puts you in your place. There is always another challenge, a bigger or smarter fish to pursue. There is always that day when you lose, and lose badly. Sometimes these are the moments you remember most clearly—when you admitted defeat but craved another chance.

The lure of saltwater fly fishing appears in many forms and environments. Some expeditions require much equipment and many dollars. Other, more modest angling adventures offer the solitude of a quiet backwater or lonely beach. Salt water offers quality angling even in the shadows of big cities.

Whether it is an ocean beach, a small backwater estuary, a shallow flat, or the open sea, the ocean offers many unique locations that provide fine fishing. In many places you can park your car, walk a little, and have a beach all to yourself—with a chance of taking the trophy of a lifetime. The fish are not always big or glamorous, but they are strong, tough, and challenging. The strength of a four-pound jack crevalle or the comparable Pacific kelp bass, would shock the sweetwater angler. There are so many species of fish in so many locations that it is hard to know where to begin. My only regret is that I will never be able to experience it all—there is too much for one lifetime.

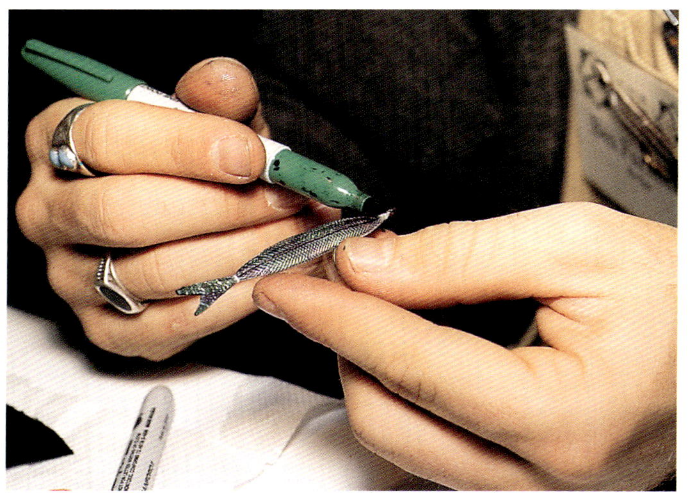

Ben Furimsky uses permanent markers to color his Shinetail Minnow.

The first anglers who caught saltwater fish probably did so by chance. Surely, salmon and trout anglers hooked other species when they fished waters that mixed with the sea. Without the proper tackle, many encounters must have ended with lost equipment and deflated egos.

Although there were a few earlier pioneers, the move to saltwater fly fishing started in the late 1940s to early 1950s. Joe Brooks first, then Lefty Kreh, Harry Kime, Jimmy Albright, Cap Calvin, A. J. McClane, and a host of others brought saltwater fly fishing into focus. It was almost 35 years ago when I read the section on salt water in Joe Brooks's *Fly Fishing.* I started saltwater fly fishing shortly thereafter.

Sight-fishing in crystal-clear, shallow water is perhaps the most exciting way to enjoy the salt. Redfish, striped bass, bluefish, barracuda, and snook are just some of the fish that feed in skinny water, but when it comes to pure flats-fishing, the bonefish is king.

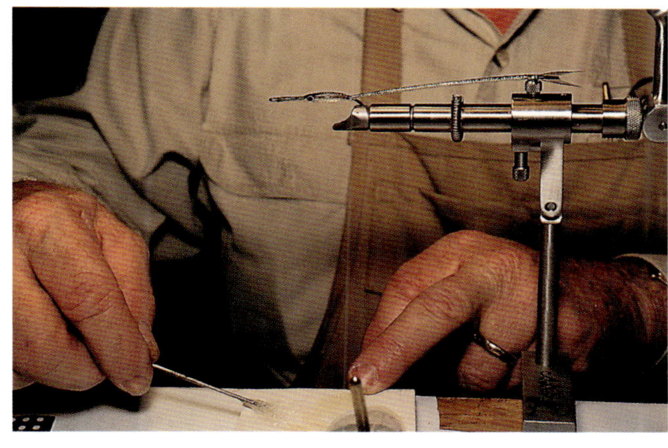

D.L. Goddard uses epoxy for the creation of his Mylar Needlefish, as well as his Mylar Minnow.

Hunting, sighting, and stalking a fish in this environment takes patience, skill, and a little luck. Doing it on your own, from vise to net, is the ultimate experience. Bonefish were the first species to bring fly rodders to skinny water, and they are certainly a challenge to the longrodder at sea, even with a guide. There are few thrills in fly fishing that can match casting to a big tailing bonefish. You first see a shadow, or a wake, then the tail cuts the water's surface, glimmering like a silver sickle. The tail flutters, producing a slapping sound; the fish is feeding, the time is right. Now you must make a quick, accurate, quiet cast or the opportunity is lost. It's you and the fish, it's exciting, and if you win one time in three it's as good as hitting .300 in baseball.

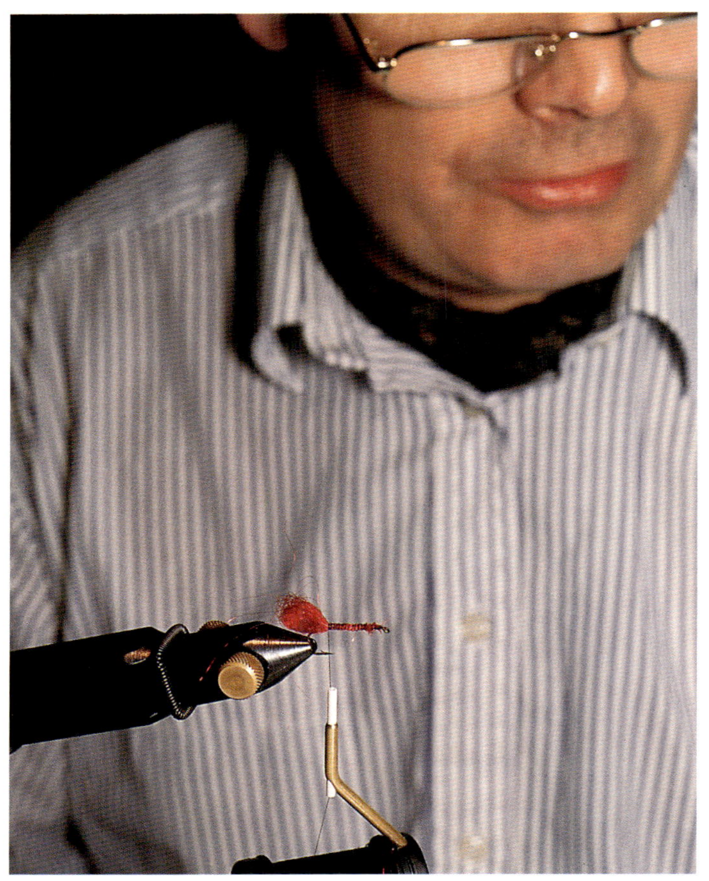

Robert Spaight, of Lincolnshire, England uses more traditional materials like fur and hackle for his wet patterns for sea-run brown trout.

Big fish on fly tackle draw anglers from all walks of life. For some it's an irresistible physical challenge: Can you beat that big fish? For others it's the awesome sight of a 100-pound-plus fish taking a fly. Billfish and tarpon are special because they're not only big, they make spectacular jumps. Both take flies readily and require teamwork and often hard work to land. Some billfishing requires selling the farm to pursue, yet each year these great fish attract many fly rodders.

The improvement in tackle has spawned the tremendous growth in saltwater fly fishing today. Many new fly patterns have been contributed by anglers joining the sport each season. With new fly-tying materials appearing faster than political promises, the number of fly patterns will continue to grow.

The simplicity of fly fishing the sea is alluring: no Latin names of bugs—or flies the size of dust. In many cases, you need only to suggest a food type. I enjoy seeing how many species in different environments will strike one fly type. For the fly-pattern nuts, though, there are thousands to choose from, and still many more waiting to be discovered.

One pleasure of saltwater fly fishing is selecting the right fly—having a few flies that work well, then adding to the fly box as you learn the secrets of a location. Whether you tie your own flies or buy them, when you select a fly and it works, it's rewarding. When you create your own successful fly, that's even better.

In the following pages, you will learn how and why different anglers developed fly patterns. This book does not just have the typical fly menu that most books contain. Instead, the author shows the personality behind each pattern. As the flies' creators come alive, their stories of ingenuity and adventure will shed light on both the flies and the habits of the fish they are designed to snare. And the flies themselves are sure to give you countless hours of sound fishing.

Enjoy.

Northeast

From the pounding surf of Long Island to the rocky coast of Maine, striped bass are the name of the game for most Northeastern saltwater fly rodders. The stripers run in numbers, close to shore, sometimes in only eight or 10 inches of water. Though not as strong or hard-fighting as some saltwater species, stripers, which run to 40 pounds, are superb for eating and have drawn squadrons of fly-rod devotees. Second to stripers in the Northeast are bluefish, which run from four to 12 pounds in these cold waters. Bluefish hunt in packs; they are savage, aggressive feeders that jump in shallow water when hooked.

The Northeast offers a tremendous variety of water for saltwater fly fishing, including quiet, inshore estuaries, rocky coves, and white sand beaches. Off Long Island's eastern tip, an established offshore fishery exists for big-game species like bluefin tuna, marlin, and shark in spots like the "Mudhole," off Block Island, and "Fingers," off Montauk.

North Atlantic waters warm only briefly during the summer and early fall, but when they do, bonito and false albacore blitz the beach, streaking inshore and decimating baitfish. Both of these extremely strong and fast offshore species can be caught from shore.

Saltwater angler Tom Piccolo says the stripers generated the initial excitement for the sport. Many a once-devout trout fisherman, he says, has forsaken the sweet water for the sight of a school of big stripers feeding on the surface inshore.

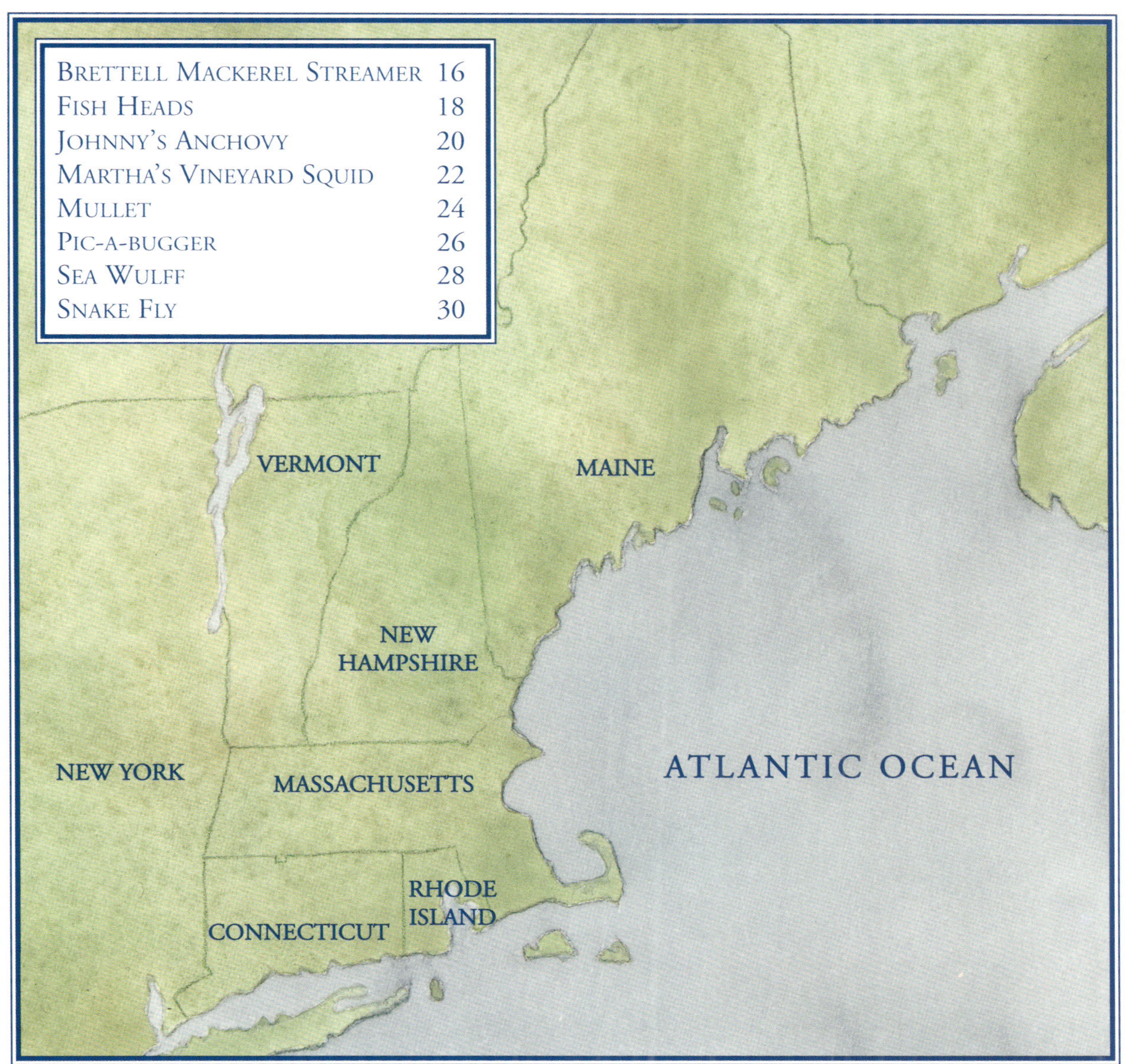

Brettell Mackerel Streamer 16
Fish Heads 18
Johnny's Anchovy 20
Martha's Vineyard Squid 22
Mullet 24
Pic-a-bugger 26
Sea Wulff 28
Snake Fly 30
VERMONT
MAINE
NEW HAMPSHIRE
NEW YORK
MASSACHUSETTS
ATLANTIC OCEAN
RHODE ISLAND
CONNECTICUT

In the early 1990s, the all-but-forgotten striped bass harvest exploded on the eastern seaboard. A fish whose population had once been perilously small was back, thanks to conservation policies dating to the 1970s. The only question facing local anglers: What to catch them with? Southern Maine guide **Steve Brettell** came up with the solution: an imitation of the mackerel.

Brettell, 39, started fly fishing for stripers 25 years ago in Massachusetts's Essex River. Today he works year-round as a guide, taking anglers after stripers and blues in the summer and fall, and hunting waterfowl during the fall. Among Brettell's favorite saltwater haunts are the islands and points around southern Maine's famous Biddeford Pool—a rocky piece of coast at the mouth of the Saco River whose fluvial food sources make it a big hunting ground.

The best time to fish stripers in New England is between June and August, as they load up on fuel for their journey to the Chesapeake for mating season, the return trip in their annual migration. Brettell surmised that a major source of food for stripers in the area was the seemingly ever-plentiful mackerel. Testing different tying materials, Brettell aimed to create the impression of the shiny, slender, dark-green striped mackerel. Surprisingly, he found his answer in the uncomplicated, green-dyed, striped chicken hackle.

Brettell likes flies that can be cast repeatedly, all day long, so a bulky fly was out. In order to keep the weight and bulk down, his secret was to construct the fly on a double-elbowed popper hook. The feathers are tied with a flat, lateral orientation to keep the fly slim and elegant. However, the three sections of the popper hook provide a fuller profile, with two feathers flush to the eye (aligned parallel to the stem), two off the middle joint (laying perpendicular), and finally two on the hook section (again laying parallel).

Some simple variations can be made easily. For a bi-color effect, use slightly darker materials on the top face, and lighter materials on the lower face. To add some flash, a single peacock strand can be tied on the middle plane. A slight amount of hackle, mallard, or merganser can be added to the face, forcing more water movement around the fly. Finally, the red head, which suggests gills or even blood, can be exaggerated somewhat and bead eyes can even be added for additional weight.

Brettell uses the fly in the darker periods of the day—early morning (5 to 10 A.M.), late evenings, and on overcast days. Subdued light seems especially critical when fished over sandbars. Generally, he fishes the fly very fast, in major two- or three-foot strips.

His gear is simple but effective. When not covering the active, churning water around the pools and rocks of a slack low tide, he frequently pursues stripers in an eighteen-foot aluminum vessel with casting platform (an Alaskan, by Lund) and two outboards, 40 hp and 15 hp. In hand, he uses a 9-weight, 9-foot graphite stick. On the reel, he suggests a shooting head, sinking tip, floating line, allowing for a five to 10 second drop before starting the strips. The leader is something unique, though. To avoid wind knots, he uses a 20 lb. to 25 lb. monofilament leader, five to six feet in length, made from a stiff worming line manufactured by Teeny, Orvis, or L.L. Bean.

Brettell Mackerel Streamer

Jack Gartside made a name for himself in the saltwater fly-tying world for, among other things, being the first person to incorporate into his fly designs the now-popular tubing material called "Corsair"—a name that evokes pirates, privateers, and their sleek, swift-sailing ships.

"I came across the material in a flea market in Amsterdam," says Gartside, 52, who drives a Boston cab when he's not tying professionally or fishing. Asked how fate brought him to an Amsterdam flea market, Gartside says, "I was taking a year off, working odd jobs here and there. I was working in a tobacco factory."

Whatever his original mission, when Gartside returned home he developed a line of flies around Corsair that he says work equally well in fresh or salt water. A friend who recognized the material told him it's used in medicine for venal reconstruction. "It's a good way to form and shape without using epoxy, which I don't enjoy," he says. "I played with it for a number of years before anyone took notice. Only with the recent interest in striper fishing has it become popular." One of the great strengths of Corsair as a tying material, says Gartside, is that it allows tiers of "modest talent" to make flies that are durable, effective, and beautiful. Its tube shape easily lends itself to minnow imitations.

The Feather-Wing and Marabou Fish Heads, which Gartside invented 10 years ago, combine the sturdy realism of a Corsair head and shoulder with a willowy, impressionistic, feathered back end. The feather and marabou create action, so the Fish Heads breathe in the water.

Gartside works the fly-fishing exposition circuit. He appears at shows clad in a blue velour smoking jacket. A poster-size black-and-white photograph at his booth shows him as a younger man, seated behind his tying table, cigarette dangling from his lips, drink at the ready.

In sluggish currents, Gartside fast-fishes the Heads. In swift rips he lets them drift. While fast-fishing, he twitches and jerks his rod tip and he's never still, covering lots of water—five or six miles a session. "I fish very quickly," he says. "I'm not a rock, jetty or boat fisherman. I move up a river with the tide. I move down with the tide. I go where the fish are."

Baseball legend Ted Williams taught Gartside to tie his first fly at the now defunct New England Sportsman's Show in Boston. "He was my idol. I was thrilled, of course. I immediately converted my old spinning rod into a fly rod."

In those early days, Gartside fly-fished the salt water north of Boston for mackerel and pollock—stripers were scarce in Northeastern waters when he was a young man. He also started fly fishing for trout; the flies he ties today are mostly for fresh water, though he personally prefers plundering the salt.

Gartside fishes all over the world—England, New Zealand, Norway, Mexico, France. But his favorite place to fish is his backyard—Boston Harbor. It's not unusual for him to have 100-fish days after long nights in his cab. One recent summer day, he says, he caught 68 stripers, all over 25 inches. "It's not quiet fishing," Gartside says. "Harbor sounds fill the air. There are tugs hooting, boats are motoring. You can hear traffic. There are airplanes taking off. But I love it."

Fish Heads

Usually the false albacore that drift into the summer-warmed waters of the Northeast are knocked out by the first cold front of October. Such has been the case along the reefs fanning out from Rhode Island's Watch Hill Lighthouse. But, in the fall of 1995, the false albacore stayed on and on, weathering three cold fronts, hunting Sugar Reef, Catumb Rock, and Napatree Point until the first week of November. "The bait kept them in. Guys who had been chasing them for years were suddenly having 20-, 25-fish days," says **Johnny Glenn**, whose Johnny's Anchovy is an uncanny mimic of the brownish bait fish that are ambrosia to the false albacore.

The rocky Watch Hill reefs are a natural killing ground for the albacore, a beautiful fish with tuna-shaped body, pearl-white belly, and olive-green back broken by blue lines. The water at the reefs is 35 to 50 feet deep, while the reefs themselves are six to 10 feet down, with exposed outcroppings. The tide sweeps the brown clouds of bait against the rocks and the powerful albacore ambush them there.

Glenn, a guide and tier in his late 30s, says that when the albacore are slashing like streaks of lightning through the bait, it's important to throw the Anchovy "right in the kitchen"—in other words, on the nose of the albacore's conical snout. "I don't believe in a fast retrieve," says Glenn. "Just a little twitch, twitch. Hopefully, the albacore will pick it out of the bait if you keep it in there long enough." Hooked, the seven- to 14-pound albacore give two or three runs of up to 100 yards. They scream along the beach. You bull them back.

Johnny's Anchovy is about two inches long, its body reddish brown superhair, a synthetic crinkled to refract light. It has pearl glimmer for flash and prismatic eyes. Glenn tried using epoxy for the Anchovy but found silicone has a more natural feel: The fish doesn't spit it out when it bites down. Silicone is also easier to work and it doesn't sink as fast as epoxy, an advantage when you want the fly lingering as long as possible in the killing zone.

Albacore, Glenn says, are the best fish the Northeast has to offer on a fly rod because of their speed and strength. They aren't good to eat—their flesh is pungent and oily. But they're stronger than bonefish and put up a better fight at the boat. "They start to bull on you and then head for the bottom," says Glenn. "It can be a real standoff."

The albacore have sharp eyesight and are leader-shy. Glenn recommends a 10- or 12-pound test in quiet water and a 16-pound fluorocarbon in faster current. He fishes the albacore with a 9- or 10-weight rod strung with a full sinking line.

On the Watch Hill reefs, the sinking line drops the Anchovy into the albacore's range; without it the fly rides current, rafting on the surface. The albacore feed by rocketing up, grabbing their quarry and then plunging back to the depths.

A commercial tier for the past few years, Glenn turned full time to the salt after giving up life as a musician and jingles composer in New York City. "I traded the city in for the ocean," he says. "I'm on the water every day. I was in New York City with a bunch of other guys chasing a million bucks. They were saying, 'In 30 years, I'm going to go fishing.' But then I said the heck with it. I'm going fishing now."

Johnny's Anchovy

Jaime Boyle raced collegiate-class sailboats when he was an undergraduate at Tulane University. He might have been on his way to the Olympics.

But at age 20, when Boyle first picked up a fly rod, his sailing days were over. "I haven't touched a sailboat since I started fishing," he says. "I got burned out on the attitudes of sailboat racers. It's weird—cutthroat. I fell in love with the whole fly-fishing attitude—everybody teaching everybody everything."

Boyle, now in his mid-20s, lives on Martha's Vineyard, or "The Rock," as he calls it, year-round. He guides and charters. And sits at the feet of Cooper Gilkes III, a Vineyard tier and tackle-shop owner.

Orvis markets Boyle's Martha's Vineyard Squid, a fly inspired by bait casters he bumped into who were pulling in stripers with dead squid on the island's Lobsterville Beach. Boyle ties the fly with six to 10 white saddle feathers, which are tied off the bend of a long-shank hook and splayed. The hook's shank is wrapped with crystal chenille and the head of the hook hanked with glimmer. Boyle applies two coats of silicone to give the fly shape. He ties the Squid on 2/0 to 4/0 hooks.

Boyle represents a new generation of fly tiers who work exclusively in salt water. He's never once dipped his line in "the sweet." And he has no desire to. Not with stripers running up and down Lobsterville Beach. Or the bluefish blasting bait off Dogfish Bar. Or the albacore streaking along the shore at Cape Pogue Gut. Or bonito blitzing the jetties at Menemsha.

Boyle is in love—and it looks like for life. Not only is he indifferent to fly fishing fresh water, he also has little interest in fishing anywhere but "The Rock." He grew up outside Boston, and his family began vacationing on the Vineyard when he was eight. "No matter how hard I tried to go away, " he explains, "I always ended up coming back. Now I'm here to stay."

The first time Boyle picked up a fly rod was six years ago, after he met a chef from the Edgartown Yacht Club who fly fished for bonito. Boyle thought that was "pretty neat, pretty wild." He got a gift certificate for a fly rod and reel. Then he met Gilkes. Boyle was on his way.

In mid-April, his beloved striped bass start running off the Gay Head side of the island. Small in the early season, they increase in size through the summer and fall. Around Memorial Day, bluefish show up. Boyle casts plugs 70 yards and lures ravenous blues to the beach.

Bonito show up in the last week of July; albacore appear at the end of August. There's a special place in Boyle's heart for the albacore. He wades and casts to them in waist-deep water. The thrill of watching them swim is unsurpassed. Their proximity is dazzling. "To be waist-deep in the water and see a tuna streaking past at 60 miles an hour, a blaze of neon green...well, that's really something," says Boyle. "It's not something you see everyday.

"An albacore will fight until its heart explodes," he says. "I've spent 25 minutes trying to revive a fish with no visible wounds."

Martha's Vineyard Squid

"Loaded for bear" is how **Bill Catherwood**, the granddaddy of Eastern saltwater fly tiers, describes going fishing with the oversized, imitative streamer patterns that recently earned him the lifetime achievement award from the Federation of Fly Fishers. The only other person ever so honored was the late fly fishing legend Lee Wulff.

Catherwood, 71, says he was "tickled pink" by the award. A loquacious fellow, he's still catching the big Northeastern stripers and bluefish that were his initial inspiration when he developed the patterns dubbed "The Giant Killers" in a 1968 Outdoor Life article. The article brought Catherwood and saltwater flies to national attention. Writer Tom McNally made it clear that here, finally, was something completely different. Catherwood was one of the first tiers to depart from impressionistic flies for salt water and tie realistic patterns to match the hatch—or, in this case, bait fish—that are fodder to saltwater predators.

"Forty years ago I went to the ocean with a trout fisherman's mentality," says Catherwood. "At first I was tying the streamers only three inches long. In kind of a hurry they grew to six or seven inches."

On the rocky shoreline north of Boston, Catherwood caught the attention of local anglers in the 1950s when he began casting his killers for stripers and bluefish. He remembers hearing things like: "There's some nut out there with a fly rod."

Not that Catherwood is exactly a fly rod purist. "My wife and I have done things for commercial trolling and jigging," he says. "We've built jigs that are over four pounds, and umbrella rigs for sport fishing that are so deadly they tried to make them illegal. It was great advertising. I couldn't take the stuff we do for a living to a fly fishing shop. We'd be drummed out of town."

When Catherwood first began tying the big streamers, there were no fly rods built to handle their weight. Helen DeSteffano of Boston built him a custom 10-weight rod on an experimental Harnell blank. Concurrently, Leon Martuche was pioneering experimental saltwater taper lines for Scientific Anglers. Fly, rod, and line all came together and the modern era of saltwater fly fishing was born.

In the yard of his home in Tewksbury, Massachusetts, Catherwood keeps chickens specially bred to produce the long hackles he needs for his six-inch patterns. He ties with only natural materials, convinced their action is superior to synthetics. He also keeps black-faced sheep, which contribute the shiny hair that rounds off so many of his flies.

The Mullet pictured here is pure Catherwood, a fly from the hands of a master. It's beautiful and enticing—a perfect artful blending of form and function. Its hair head, like those on most flies Catherwood ties these days, is trimmed from front to back, creating a rippling effect when the fly is stripped through the water. "I want the blunt bullet nose to bust the water," Catherwood says. "When that happens, small turbulence flows over the head and over the wing, activating it."

The biggest names in saltwater fly tying acknowledge the debt they owe Catherwood. Dan Blanton "always tries to emulate" Catherwood. George Roberts Jr. notes that tiers are forever "discovering" things Catherwood was already doing 30 years ago. Lefty Kreh sums it up, calling Catherwood "a legend."

Mullet

Tom Piccolo wanted a fly that imitated striped bass baits. He also wanted a fly that was easy to tie and easy to cast. He found the answer to both needs in an adaptation of a popular freshwater fly: The marabou-and-chenille body of Piccolo's Pic-a-Bugger ties in a flash, and its low wind resistance makes throwing it a snap.

"I took the Wooly Bugger and used more marabou for the tail," says Piccolo. "I put on a salmon collar to get more bulk up front. I tied the fly in chartreuse, which I'd read was a color that really excited stripers." He also adds red thread on the head to give the impression of gills. He ties the fly on a 2 or 0 sized hook. The traditional freshwater bugger is about one inch long; Piccolo's is two to three inches.

Piccolo designed the Bugger to be fished primarily in western Long Island Sound. The fly has also proven effective all along the East Coast, and Piccolo, his friends, and customers have successfully used the Pic-a-Bugger in Alaska and Tierra del Fuego, Argentina, as well.

Piccolo fishes the fly in two ways. Normally, he gives it three strips of six to 18 inches, followed by a pause. The fly pulsates through the water, giving the impression of an injured baitfish trying to escape, exhausting itself and then panicking. If the Bugger is fished in a strong current or a rip, however, Piccolo just lets it drift.

From shore, Piccolo uses an intermediate line and a six- to seven-foot leader. From a boat in deeper water or in a heavy current or rip, he throws a 300- to 350-gram sinking head line with a short leader, no more than four feet long. "You want to get the fly down quick and keep it down," he says.

The Pic-a-Bugger is used primarily to imitate sand eels and small alewives. It also works well when grass shrimp—the small, clear shrimp that live in marshes and float around during high tide—are present. At night, Piccolo dresses the bugger in black. It can be tied with a fluorescent red body and fluorescent yellow head—an effective variation during the cinder worm hatch.

Piccolo, 48, resides in New Orleans and is general manager of The Sporting Life, a full Orvis dealer. He also conducts fly-tying and fly-casting demonstrations and classes on both the East and West Coasts. He started tying in 1972, fishing for brown and rainbow trout in the Housatonic and Farmington Rivers in northwest Connecticut, where he grew up. He started tying for salt water in 1975.

Today, he fishes both fresh and salt, but he prefers salt water. He explains why: "They're all native fish. There's no stocking. And you have no idea what you're going to catch. It could be a striped bass, a bluefish, albacore or bonito. And you never know when you're going to hook into a 20-pound fish."

Piccolo caught a 42-pound striper in 1987 with a Pic-a-Bugger. He was casting from shore in Larchmont, New York. It was daybreak, high tide, calm and overcast. Piccolo slung the Pic-a-Bugger into one of the breaks. A striper hit, and at first didn't put up much of a fight. Piccolo had no idea of its size. Then it rolled on the surface and Piccolo's mouth went dry. The fish took off, straight into the Sound. "Thank God all my mechanical gear was working," says Piccolo. "Thank God I was able to land it."

Pic-a-bugger

Lee Wulff was always ahead of the pack. One of the earliest proponents of catch-and-release, he was quoted as saying, "A good game fish is too valuable to catch only once." Whether it was a fashion controversy like wearing his vest outside his clothes or an unheard-of display of ingenuity like catching a 10-pound salmon without a rod (he used only line, reel, and fly), Wulff is as responsible as any other person for the face of fly fishing today. When he died in a plane crash in 1991 at the age of 86, Wulff left a legacy of highly effective flies and equally prominent theories about how they should be used.

"You don't measure pleasure in fishing by pounds," he said before his death in an interview with f-stop Fitzgerald. "You measure it by the challenge it gives you. Small fish that are challenging can give you a fishing problem. Which is what you want."

Less well-known than his classic Catskill designs like the Royal Wulff and the entire Wulff series are his saltwater designs.

"His idea was welding," says his widow Joan, herself a competition-level caster. "Welding was new at the time. It eliminated nuts and bolts. It would make for a faster production line." In a process he patented in 1952, Wulff used an injection-molding machine and a granular-type plastic to put bodies on hooks. After taking the body from the mold, he applied a solvent and embedded materials like fur, feathers, and tinsel into the body.

"He could use whatever materials he wanted," says Joan. "It was a great idea, but it never really caught on. The problem was the average tier had to buy the body from us. Fly tiers are not used to working with solvents."

When Wulff developed the plastic body fly style there was controversy over whether the flies were flies at all, or whether they should more properly be characterized as lures. Wulff defended the flies in "Flies of the Future," a 1986 article by Silvio Calabi in *Fly Rod & Reel*: "A fly is a lure that doesn't move by itself, that has no diving lip or anything to give it action; the action should come from the guy on the rod. And it must be something that can be cast on a fly rod with a fly line—cast and false-cast several times, not just heaved out there."

The molds that Wulff made for the flies are in the process of being upgraded, and Joan and her son, Douglas Cummings, who runs Royal Wulff Products, will again produce the Sea Wulff.

Using an early version of the Sea Wulff, the master landed a still-standing world-record 148-pound striped marlin off the coast of Ecuador in 1967. He was using a $12.50 rod and a reel with no drag. "I was on a small boat. I cast. I hooked him and played him four and a half hours," Wulff said. "Setting a record...breaking new ground—it's exciting to do it."

He would know.

Sea Wulff

"It's my mainstay, my workhorse," **Lou Tabory** says of his Snake Fly.

Tabory, 50, the Connecticut-based author of *Inshore Fly Fishing* and *Lou Tabory's Guide to Saltwater Baits and Their Imitations*, first tied a proto-Snake in 1980, when he was fishing the Wood River in Alaska for rainbow trout, silver salmon, and Arctic char. It was late summer, cold and gray. Tabory spotted a big 'bow and crossed the river below it. He tried several other flies before tying on the proto-Snake. When he did, the 10-pound 'bow homed in like a heat-seeking missile.

The next spring, Tabory trotted the Snake out while casting for stripers and bluefish on Long Island Sound near Westport, Connecticut. When fished against a jetty, the Snake "breathes" in the water, Tabory says, so you can let the fly wallow and drift without a retrieve, allowing for a long presentation in the strike zone. Any long, soft fiber works well for the Snake's tail, but Tabory prefers ostrich herl, which gives the fly extra length and excellent action.

He also can modify the Snake to match the cinder worm hatch, that strange mating dance that occurs along the Atlantic Coast, mostly at night, at the full and new moon. The cinder worm, also called the Nereid worm or clam worm, is common live bait in the Northeast and is bottom-fished for flounder. The worm is brilliantly colored, orange and green, and inhabits the seaboard from Maine to the Carolinas, burrowing in soft mud or sand. Wriggling from their sea-mulch beds, the worms spawn on calm, still nights, swirling around each other in a dense, undulating cloud, each spiraling downward to the ocean floor. Tabory fishes the swarms along shore and in estuaries.

During its mating dance, the cinder worm sheds part of its body. The cinder measures three to 15 inches before spawning, two-and-a-half to four inches afterward. Tabory's Snake is tied to match the cinders' smaller phase.

Fishing stripers during the hatch, Tabory says, can be frustrating—or fantastic. It all depends on how many worms are in the water and how long the fish have been feeding. If there's a glut of bait, the artificial may be lost in the feeding frenzy.

Tabory had no such misfortune one night several years back. The place: Ash Creek, where it empties into the Sound in Fairfield, Connecticut. A friend had been out in the swarm the night before and told Tabory stripers were pounding the bait but he hadn't scored. At about 10:30 P.M., they launched a small runabout. The water of the estuary was seven to eight feet deep, the tide high and outgoing.

"It was a balmy June night," Tabory recalls. "Flat, calm, and dead still. We spotted feeding fish right off the ramp. We could see them boiling on the surface. We could hear them. They made a splashing, sipping, popping sound."

Tabory tied a black Snake to his floating line and 12-pound tippet, heaving short casts off his 10-weight rod into the Creek's effluence. The Snake slithered on the surface. As it swung around, the stripers hit.

"It was like nymphing for trout," Tabory says. "Fish were breaking around us in the marsh." The fish weren't large—all under 10 pounds. But Tabory caught 10 of them—brisk action for 90 minutes.

Snake Fly

Mid-Atlantic

Halfway up the Atlantic coast, the cold Labrador and warm Gulf Stream currents converge to create a marine environment friendly to both cold- and warm-water species of fish. From the rocking surf of the New Jersey shore to the secluded Spatina grass flats behind Charleston, South Carolina, the mid-Atlantic region offers saltwater fly rodders a vast range of prey in a dizzying array of water.

Eighty miles off the Jersey shore, anglers like IGFA record-holder Bill Hayes plumb the Hudson and Wilmington canyons with fast-sinking lines for bluefin and yellowfin tuna. Closer to shore, stripers and bluefish hunt the surf line or sweep through shallow estuaries.

Chesapeake fly rodders have witnessed an enormous influx of striped bass in the last five years. Cobia are also caught in the Bay's mouth, and veteran mid-Atlantic fly caster Tom Earnhardt says there are reports that tarpon have been sighted and hooked there as well.

Off Cape Hatteras, the Gulf Stream runs closer to the continent than any place north of Florida. Here anglers are plucking giant bluefin tuna and billfish from the Stream 10 to 20 miles offshore.

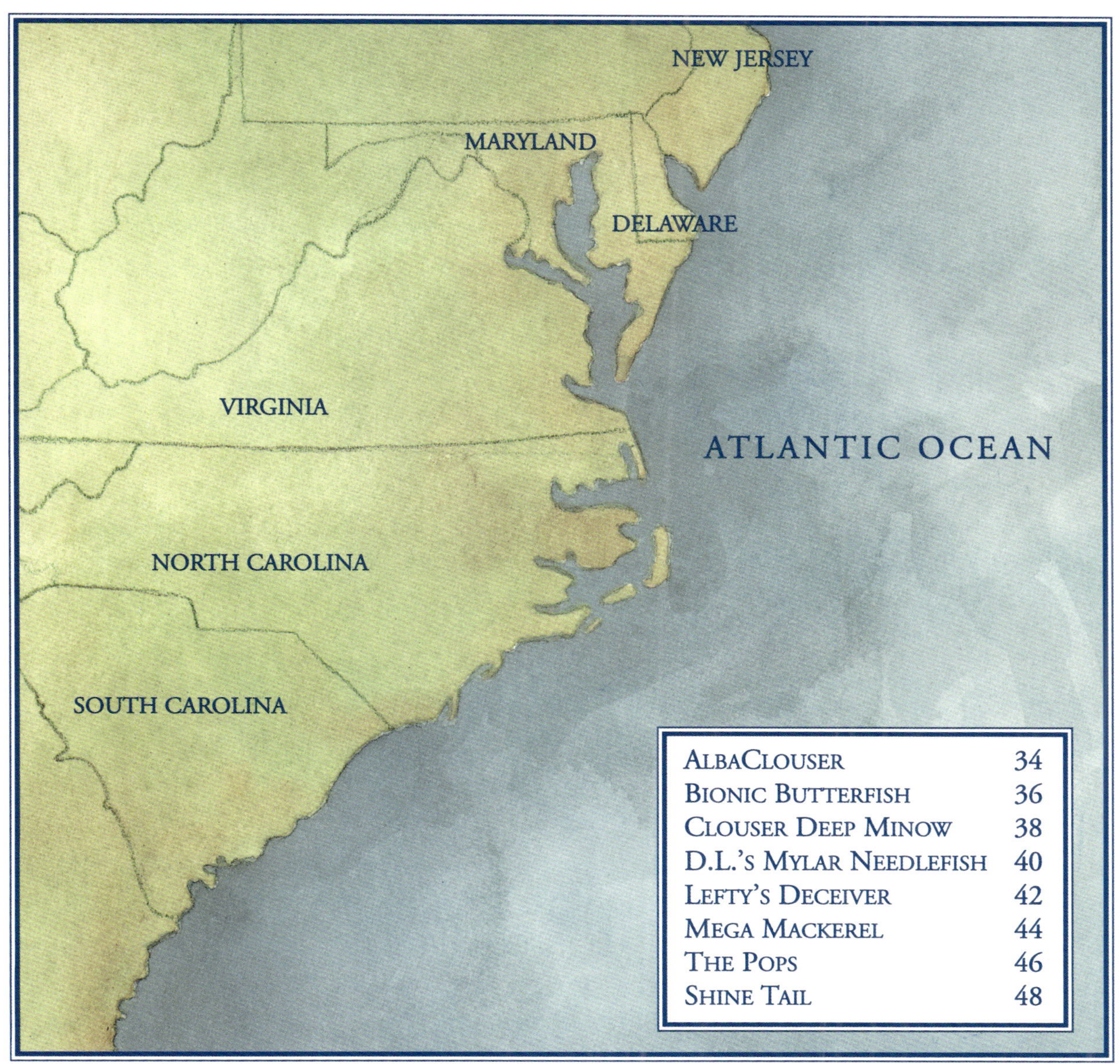
NEW JERSEY
MARYLAND
DELAWARE
VIRGINIA
ATLANTIC OCEAN
NORTH CAROLINA
SOUTH CAROLINA

Tom Earnhardt's AlbaClouser is one of the major producers on the North Carolina coast for false albacore, bonito, and Spanish mackerel. It's a variation of Bob Clouser's Deep Minnow, but it's tied with synthetic materials rather than the bucktail used in Clouser's originals. The super-synthetic nylons, Earnhardt says, help create a fly with the translucence and flash of a live minnow.

Earnhardt, a 50-year-old law professor and author of *Fly Fishing the Tidewaters*, acknowledges most of his saltwater fly patterns are derivations in one way or another. "I do have my own patterns, but I respect the pioneer tiers—the Krehs, Blantons, Clousers, and others," he says. "Most flies are just variations on their themes."

The AlbaClouser mimics bay anchovy, Spanish sardine, and spearing—all slender minnows, one and a half to four inches long, that are generically referred to as glass minnows or silversides. Earnhardt ties his imitations on hook sizes 1/0 to 4, using three variations for different water conditions. The flies' eyes, like the naturals', are painted silver with a black dot. And like Clouser's originals, all styles of the AlbaClouser are virtually "weedless," rarely snagging weeds or rocks, because the weight of their lead eyes keeps the hooks turned upward.

Earnhardt, who has been fly fishing the shores of North Carolina for 30 years, has a home on Cape Lookout on the Outer Banks, two miles from the Cape Lookout lighthouse. Teaching duties at North Carolina Central University keep him anchored in Raleigh, but he fishes the Outer Banks 10 months out of the year.

The Bight at Cape Lookout and adjoining beaches near Earnhardt's home have hundreds of acres of flats where albacore come in from mid-October through November to feed on glass minnows and finger mullet. Lookout's myriad beaches have endless nooks and crannies. Earnhardt says he can always find a lee shore from which to cast.

Fly fishing in salt water isn't necessarily more complicated than freshwater fly rodding, says Earnhardt, but what he loves most about salt water is the variety of conditions. "When conditions seem next to impossible, you can often make it work," he says. "Fishing with flies is often an advantage and not a hindrance."

The variety of saltwater game and bait species also never fails to astound him. You can go out looking for silversides, he says, and run into menhaden or mullet. "You go to a wreck expecting amberjack," he adds, "and instead you find big barracuda.

"You have to match the hatch the same way you do in a stream for trout," Earnhardt says. "In the same way you need good presentation on a stream, you need it in salt water. Often what's critical on a stream is a drag-free float—dead drift. In salt water you have to move your fly at the right speed and cadence. You don't move a shrimp pattern at Mach 1. Shrimp don't move that fast. You have to study the basic biology of the critters you are imitating."

Alba Clouser

The charter captains would laugh at me and hang up when I told them I wanted to catch tuna on a fly rod," says **Bill Hayes**. "They don't laugh anymore."

That's because Hayes showed that it could be done. He started fly fishing for bluefin and yellowfin tuna in the bluewater canyons 80 to 100 miles off the New Jersey coast in 1986 and has since racked up three different tippet-class world records for tuna: a 30-pound bluefin in 1992, a 52-pound yellowfin in 1993, and a 68-pound yellowfin in 1994.

In the spring of '96, Hayes and the Bionic headed out to Diamond Shoals off Cape Hatteras, where people have hooked 40 bluefin tuna a day, each weighing between 300 to 800 pounds. There, some anglers take giant tuna with 10-pound bluefish. "Basically you want to throw at them the biggest, baddest fly you can cast," Hayes says.

The plump, glittering white-and-silver Bionic weds Ralph Kantz's Mylar Minnow and a big Deceiver. Hayes developed the fly because a standard Deceiver's six-hackle tail didn't present enough of a silhouette to the deep-feeding tuna. Hayes rigs the fly on tandem 5-0 and 3-0 hooks, which he sharpens, filing away the barbs. "All the barb does is keep the hook from going all the way in," he says, "and makes it harder to release the fish safely."

White saddle feathers comprise the Bionic's tail, with a combination pearl and silver firefly tinsel on top and pearl and flashabou below. Twelve more hackles flesh out the fly's body. A big clump of bucktail is used for the collar.

The Bionic's girth should suggest something fleshy, hefty, and delicious to the tuna. "The fly should be as big as the palm of your hand," says Hayes, "as big as you can make it."

When Hayes started fishing tuna with a fly rod, there weren't rods or tackle on the market that could handle the sport. It took him 30 minutes to land his first fish, a 30-pounder, which he brought to the boat exhausted and spent. Now he lands most fish under 50 pounds in 10 minutes or less.

Hayes angles for tuna with a Gary Loomis 15-weight MEGA rod, Abel No. 5 reel, spectra backing, deep-water express line, and 20-pound fluorocarbon leaders. "I will go after them with those leaders until I have records that are tough to beat," he says. "Then I will go after them on smaller stuff."

Over the canyons off New Jersey, Hayes chunks butterfish around the boat and spots the approaching tuna on sonar. Sometimes the tuna appear on the sonar like comets streaking through the bait. Hayes uses long casts and feathers his line to sink the fly down into the tuna's range.

Hayes, 33, who owns the Angler's Pro Shop in Souderton, Pennsylvania, admits that his preoccupation with fly rodding for tuna is both expensive and exhausting. "I don't know," he sighs. "Some guys get hooked on drugs, food, sex. I tell you what: I've been hooked on fishing since I was a little kid. First, I wanted to catch lots of fish. Then catch big fish. Then quality fish."

Quality fish is what led Hayes to tuna. He says they are the hardest-fighting fish in the sea. "They're shaped like torpedoes, and pure muscle," he says. "For brute strength, nothing comes close. They never give up. Never."

Bionic Butterfish

The legendary Lefty Kreh says if he had but one saltwater fly to use for the rest of his days, it would be the Clouser Deep Minnow.

"I don't know how I developed it, but I know why I developed it," says **Bob Clouser**, 57. "I was striving to get a better minnow imitation that did not necessarily look like a minnow but acted like one."

Ironically, the Deep Minnow, though revered in saltwater fly fishing circles, was developed in 1985 for smallmouth bass in Pennsylvania's Susquehanna River. Kreh was the person who first championed the fly for salt. "He was the first person to take it out of Pennsylvania. He used it and promoted it and it's taken off ever since," says Clouser, who owns a fly fishing shop in Middletown, Pennsylvania.

By trial and error, Clouser arrived at the key to the fly's performance—its lead eyes are tied up front on the hook, causing the fly to move with the head-sinking, darting action of a wounded bait fish. The concentration of weight up front quickens the fly's action and causes it to move headfirst wherever it goes. "The fly never stops moving," says Clouser. "Even when it's not being retrieved, it falls or turns to the side."

From his shop, Clouser sells 16 color variations of the Deep Minnow. He uses eight himself. Tops on his list is a chartreuse-and-white combination, though he might use darker shades for a particularly bright day.

Clouser ties the minnow in a broad range of sizes, from a No. 10 to a 7/0 saltwater hook. He uses deer hair for the tails of the larger flies, but for smaller sizes he'll tie in guard hair from rabbits, fox, or raccoon.

Clouser has used the minnow in the Yucatan for bonefish, permit, jack crevalle, and barracuda of up to 40 inches. "They're super fast, with treacherous teeth," he says of the barracudas. "They destroy the fly. One fly, one fish."

Off the New Jersey shore, Clouser has caught albacore, striped bass, and bluefish with the Deep Minnow. In the Chesapeake and North Carolina, he's taken grey trout, flounder, and sand shark with the fly.

While most people think the Deep Minnow is "weedless," that's not strictly true, says Clouser: The fly's beady eyes can snag on rocks. But since the fly's hook faces up, most fish are hooked in the roofs of their mouths, with very few hookups in gills or tongue.

Clouser, now 57, took up fly fishing on the Susquehanna when he was 14, growing up near Harrisburg. He opened his fly shop in 1980 after losing his job of 26 years in Acme Markets' Meat Department when the chain closed its local stores.

"It was either go to work for myself or go to work for somebody else," says Clouser. "I was spurred into this business by Lefty. And I have no regrets."

Clouser Deep Minnow

Goddard's fly mimics its namesake. Long and thin, with a rapierlike nose, the needlefish bobs about, hugging the surface. It is prey to a wide variety of predators, including striped bass.

With his lifelike fly, **D. L. Goddard**, 55, a retired Miami Beach police officer and former South Florida fishing guide, pulls stripers from the waters of Chesapeake Bay near his home in Easton, Maryland, where the stripers' resurgence, he says, has been phenomenal, especially in the past five years.

"You see schools of fish out there a mile long," he says. "Three years ago [1992] we had big fish, up to 45 inches. This year the fish were smaller. A 30-inch fish was a good fish."

The size of the stripers running in the Chesapeake varies from year to year, Goddard thinks, because of commercial fishing pressure. Goddard, who fished commercially as a young man, says a big net can wipe out an entire school of fish. Like the vast majority of saltwater fly rodders, Goddard is now in favor of sportfish designation for stripers. But because he knows firsthand what the stakes are in the industry, he has some sympathy for commercial fishermen.

"I know what they're going through," he says. "But the new multi-strand monofilament nets are too efficient. The fish can't see them at all. Once they're in the water they're invisible. They're deadly. The electronic gear is very sophisticated. And they have airplanes to seine around whole schools. They do that, it's gone. They don't have the right to go out and destroy the fishery. That's what they're doing. Their attitude is: What can I get today?"

Goddard's weapon of choice for the stripers is a fly tied on fine mylar tubing with a No. 2 long shank hook and a black hackle tail. Two-thirds of the fly's four to six inches is body; the rest, bill. Goddard colors the whole fly with a green, permanent marking pencil. The bottom is silver or pearl. D. L.'s Mylar Needlefish is licensed with Umpqua, the biggest manufacturer of tying materials.

The best time to fish the Needle is daybreak or dusk. Hunted by osprey and eagles, stripers spook in the shallows in full light. Goddard usually fishes the fly on a floating line, keeping it as close to the surface as possible. He prefers fishing shallow shorelines—reefs, rocks, jetties, and docks that draw baitfish and bass. He strips the fly at a moderate pace, shortening his strips if he senses pursuit, giving a short hand strike so the Needle is still within range if missed on the first take.

On Maryland's eastern shore, Goddard fishes the Chop Tank River, the Little Chop Tank, and their tributaries. He knows commercial netters who work the area and have caught stripers that are over 100 pounds.

"That's a big fish," he says. "They come into the Chesapeake to spawn. They're not common, but I know they're in there. Nobody's caught one with hook and line."

Asked if he'd like to bag one of these bruisers, Goddard considers.

"When I was a kid I wanted to show everyone how many fish I caught," he says. "But as I've gotten older that doesn't matter anymore. I don't believe in tournaments and trophies. Human beings will do just about anything when you dangle lots of money in front of their noses. And that's not what fishing is about."

D. L.'s Mylar Needlefish

"I am 72 years old and I've flunked retirement," says **Lefty Kreh**, the creator of the single most popular saltwater fly, Lefty's Deceiver—a fly whose familiar image has even graced a U.S. postage stamp. With the 1991 death of Lee Wulff, Kreh, who still travels the globe fishing and lecturing, is perhaps the best-known angling personality in the world today.

Kreh does not confine himself to saltwater fly fishing—but it's in this field that he has made his deepest mark. His groundbreaking book, *Fly Fishing in Salt Water*, originally published around 1970 and reissued in 1986, is the most extensive book on the subject.

A staff contributor to numerous fishing magazines, Kreh also consults for L.L. Bean, Scientific Anglers, and Sage, among other prominent tackle manufacturers. Everyone wants a piece of Kreh: He gives more than 40 fishing demonstrations a year. One week he's in Pensacola, Florida, firing up members of the newly founded Gulf Coast Fly Fishing Club. The next he's in Henrietta, New York, leading seminars on "How to Strike a Fish" and "Dry Fly Fishing Concepts" for the annual meeting of the state's chapter of Trout Unlimited.

Kreh is known as one of the best fly casters in the country. Standing 5 feet, 7 inches tall and weighing 190 pounds, he is built, it has been said, like a gorilla—a gorilla with finesse. The length and accuracy of his casts is legendary. Like Wulff, he's able to throw a fly line without a rod, using only his hands.

"I used to do that years ago, but haven't done it in a long time," Kreh says. "It isn't as hard as it sounds. Basically, you're just double-hauling."

Born in Frederick, Maryland, Kreh has spent most of his life in the Chesapeake Bay area. He developed the Deceiver in 1958 with Tom Cofield, outdoor editor of the *Baltimore News-American* newspaper. The fly imitated the alewife, a prevalent baitfish in the bay and a favorite food of striped bass.

The first Deceiver was a four-inch-long, all-white fly with a feather wing and bucktail collar. After a year fishing the Deceiver, Kreh began experimenting with different color combinations and sizes, adding red at the throat to imitate gills—"an attack trigger," he says—and peacock herl to the top.

Kreh has fished the Deceiver all over the world. In the waters of Australia and Southeast Asia he has cast the fly to exotic species like barramundi, a snook-like fish that is prized for its flesh and commercially farmed in Thailand. "The barramundi looks like a snook, acts like a snook, and tastes like a snook," says Kreh. "They get to over 50 pounds. Thirty pounds is the biggest I know that's been taken on a fly. Like snook, they're structure-oriented. They hang out around sunken trees in rivers and ambush their food."

In *Fly Fishing in Salt Water*, Kreh describes what drew him to the salt: "Saltwater fish are much stronger than their freshwater counterparts. The freshwater fly rodder worries that a fish may break his leader—the saltwater man occasionally wonders if he owns enough line to hold the fish streaking through the water with his fly in its mouth. No one can describe the run of a bonefish, the slugging battle of a jack crevalle, the mighty leap of a tarpon; these things have to be experienced. Once they are, the freshwater angler is never the same."

Lefty's Deceiver

Sometimes it's the one that got away you remember best," says **Bill Hayes**.

The one Hayes remembers is a tenacious wahoo he hooked 50 or 60 miles out from Magdelina Bay, Mexico, a famed angling venue 200 miles north of the Baja Peninsula's Cabo San Lucas. Hayes and crew had set sail six days earlier aboard the *Patriot*, a 65-foot, custom, long-range fishing boat. Trolling the kelp paddies on the water's surface had yielded "four and a half days of awesome marlin fishing" before the group's luck began to slacken.

The kelp paddies, clusters of enmeshed yellow-green seaweed, can be as big as football fields or as small as garbage can lids. They're the only thing out there in the big blue off Magdelina—crystal-clear water 1,500 fathoms deep. Baitfish seek shelter from the tropical sun beneath the bobbing seaweed umbrellas, drawing big predators like magnets, in this case wahoo and dolphin fish.

At the outset of the trip, the Patriot had scored big on the paddies—90 wahoo in seven days. But then rough weather dispersed the kelp, and sightings from the *Patriot*'s 40-foot lookout tower became few and far between. Soon Hayes and his cronies were motoring around and around in the middle of nowhere, praying for kelp.

Finally, a kelp paddy appeared, no bigger than a small car. The *Patriot* circled it, throwing out a big Marauder—14 or 15 inches long, five inches deep, made of wood, with a bunch of hooks sprouting off it. A 15-pound dolphin and a 70-pound wahoo hit the plug. The boat was thrown into neutral and live mackerel poured into the water from the wells.

"When the mackerel hit the water they run for their lives," says Hayes. "One of the crew has to keep the fish hooked on the plug out of the way. We immediately throw flies out on a fast-sinking line, letting them sink and then drawing them back with a slow retrieve."

Hayes had tied on his Mega Mackerel, a plump fly bulked out with silver, green, and blue flashabou, firefly, and bucktail, that resembles a mackerel. He and two other anglers, both also using mackerel imitations, cast lines alongside the kelp. All three immediately hooked wahoo in the 60-pound range.

"The other guys' wahoo took off," says Hayes. "Your usual 300-to 400-yard screaming run. Wahoo usually do that. They explode off the block. If you survive that run you have an excellent chance of landing fish. I don't know why mine didn't run. He maybe went 50 yards. Then he just dug in and fought me, piss and vinegar, nose to nose. We beat the crap out of each other. He would not run. We're talking about a fish over 6 feet long. He would not quit. He would not give up. Finally, he straightened my 5/0 hook and was gone."

On that round, the anglers went 0-for-3. One guy lost his fish on the run. The other had his 100-pound test wire cut.

Then Hayes and his party went in search of more kelp.

Mega Mackerel

Richard Whitner called his popper "The Pops" for all the dads who ever took their kids fishing. Those dads would be gratified to know that a wide variety of fish, including sea trout, redfish, jack crevalle, and baby tarpon take the Pops with alacrity off the southern Atlantic Coast and in the gulf waters of Florida.

"I wanted to acknowledge the fathers who had passed on their learning," said Whitner, whose dad, a respected banker in their hometown in the mountains of northern New Jersey, helped get Whitner into a Trout Unlimited fly-tying class when he was just 10. The age requirement for the class was 11.

Whitner, a precocious tier, was on his way. The class began what has become his life's work, tying flies and working in the fishing field. "My dad tried in every way to promote and support my interest in fishing," he said. "My father let me live my dreams out. He bought me my first fly rod."

Today, Whitner, 36, lives in New Orleans and is assistant manager of The Sporting Life, a full Orvis dealer, does fly-tying demos on the outdoor and fishing exposition circuit, and struggles to make a name for himself in the ballooning billion-dollar-a-year fishing industry.

The world of a professional fly tier has its ups and downs. "Good companies are paying royalties," Whitner says. "But people are taking credit for patterns that aren't theirs. It can be disheartening. It's as if somebody took Theodore Gordon's Quill Gordon and claimed it as their own. It's a pity because it's destroying our history."

Whitner first got interested in saltwater fly fishing when the owner of a Lake Hopatcong sports shop asked him to tie tarpon flies. He was just 13 years old. "I was one of the few fly tiers in the area at the time. Tarpon flies are fairly straight forward," Whitner says.

Whitner really got interested in saltwater flies when his parents retired to Clearwater, Florida, near Tampa. Watching saltwater master tiers like Bob Popovics work was inspiring. He started fooling around with Flexo, the material used for the body of the Pops and several other Whitner flies.

Flexo, says Whitner, is woven nylon or nylon and mylar, similar to competitors' braided tubing, but its diameter can expand. The Pops is tied with jointed tail so it produces constant movement, even when drifting. The worm rattle is made with plastic instead of the more traditional glass, which breaks, or aluminum, which corrodes.

Whitner says a true popper should emulate "a bait fish fleeing over the surface from its prey." He says it's essential to "feel the fish" and wait for him to "to be on his way down" before you set the hook. This eliminates false strikes.

Doug Swisher, co-author with Carl Richards of the successful books *Selective Trout* and *Fly Fishing Strategy*, was the happy recipient of a few sample Pops. Swisher says he's caught snapper, snook, jack crevalle, baby tarpon, and ladyfish on the Pops, which mimics a shad, herring, or silverside. He pumps the fly in one to three feet of water in the "back country," shallows bordering the Gulf of Mexico near Naples, Florida. "It's a unique new process in tying," says Swisher of Whitner's work.

The Pops

Bugskin, one of the newest materials to appear on the market for tying saltwater flies, is a light leather. It can provide a remarkably realistic silhouette, and, of course, it is as durable as hide.

"It's real tough," says **Ben Furimsky**, tier of the Bugskin-based Shine Tail, a generic minnow. "I've caught over six bluefish on one fly. Usually after you catch one bluefish your fly is torn to shreds."

Developed by Furimsky's father, Chuck, who owns a leather store, the Bugskin is used to create the Shine Tail's interior body. It represents shiners and silversides along the New Jersey coast where the younger Furimsky, now in his mid-20s, fishes most of the year. In smaller sizes, it replicates rain fish, so called because when they appear in big schools they dimple the surface like rain.

"It's a great fly for the clear waters of the Northeast, where silhouette is important," Furimsky says of the Shine. "It's got a fantastic shape. But of course it doesn't have the action of feather flies."

Bugskin, which is distributed nationally to fly shops by Intertac, comes in four basic color schemes: naturals, pearlized, flash, and wild naturals. Furimsky refers to one flash Shine Tail as his Jerry Garcia, because of its tie-dye hues. Furimsky inserts the Bugskin body in Corsair tubing. Seen through Corsair webbing, the flash Bugskin looks like scales.

A former ski instructor and a recent graduate of Penn State with a degree in engineering, Furimsky also reps Bugskin at fly fishing expositions. It was at Penn State that his father, himself an alumnus of the school, was introduced to fly fishing by the well-known fly fishing author George Harvey.

During the spring, summer, and fall, the young Furimsky is out at the family's house in Ocean City, New Jersey, fly fishing the coastal water three to five times a week. He has caught striped bass, bluefish, weakfish, false albacore, and bonito on the Shine Tail. In the tropics, his father has taken snook and barracuda on the fly.

Furimsky says New Jersey water doesn't compare well with other Eastern saltwater fly fishing venues. "Overall, the water isn't what you'd like," he laments. "It's often cloudy and discolored. Our weather is rougher, and we have more slop in the water. You really have to know where to go. In clear water, fish like striped bass can see the fly at a distance and follow it. Here you have to know exactly where to put the fly."

Furimsky fishes stripers straight through the spring and summer, into the fall. Come December, when the striper season slows down, he heads for the ski slopes, often out West.

He admits striper fishing is an obsession. "Many nights I'm out there from dusk till dawn," he says. "When I started fishing at night a whole different world opened up. I came back to places I explored as a kid and they were completely different at night. The bait were in different places and so were the big fish. It was like hunting. And when you get a hit you never know if it's a 12-inch fish or a 50-pounder. It's a rush, because it could always be the big one."

Shine Tail

Florida Keys

The cachet of the Florida Keys as a saltwater fly fishing destination is unrivaled. The Keys established their reputation as the saltwater fly fisherman's mecca in the 1940s and '50s on three species: bonefish, tarpon, and permit. These fish are usually pursued by sight-casting in crystalline shallows on the flats, cays and estuaries that lace through and enfold the Keys. Fishermen wade the flats or pole over the "skinny" water in specially designed boats that skim the surface.

Captain Harry Spear, who has guided in the Keys since the early 1970s, advances the notion that the finest saltwater fly fishermen in the world either live in the Keys or trained there. He thinks the Keys are the defining saltwater fly fishery.

"It is the hardest fishery in the world," says Spear. "You're at the mercy of the fish and the elements and your own level of expertise."

Fly fishing has exploded in the Keys in the last two decades. Spear says there are up to 600 guides today; when he started, there were fewer than 60. Captain Ralph Delph, who has been instrumental in developing the offshore fly rod fishery here, agrees that Key West is the place to be for serious saltwater fly rodders.

"More world records have been caught off Key West than anywhere else in the world," he says. "Amberjack, 103 pounds. Barracuda, 37 pounds. Cobia, 83 pounds...and I'm going alphabetically."

FLORIDA
GULF OF MEXICO
Bonefish Special 52
Buchanan Special 54
Chernobyl Crab 56
Flats Master 58
Hot Lips 60
Marquesa Sunrise Special 62

When Miami angler **Chico Fernandez** came up with the Bonefish Special in 1968, he didn't know it mimicked one of the bonefish's primary forage foods. He had simply been looking at existing minnow-imitation bonefish flies, and particularly liked the coloration of the Frankie Belle, a fly from the early 1950s. What distinguished Fernandez's fly at the time was its wrap of monofilament over Mylar. Fernandez was unaware that another Florida tier, Carl Hanson, had come up with the monofilament body at the same time.

"I started to think in terms of the white, yellow, orange," he says. "The fly came out quickly and worked extremely well on the outside flats close to the channels—flats with a light color and hard bottom."

Though Fernandez didn't know it then, the Special looked to the bonefish like a young schoolmaster snapper, a fish that grows to an average size of about six pounds, but when young is only an inch or an inch and a half long. The schoolmaster has multiple yellowish bars running vertically on its sides, and many also have a single black diagonal black stripe on their heads. Mangrove snapper and amberjack have this black marking as well.

Now a well-known sportsman at 53, Fernandez was little more than an enthusiast when he created the Special. He had taken up fly fishing 13 years earlier, at age 15, on his father's yacht in Cuba. He reminisces fondly about the bamboo bonefish fly rod that got him hooked. "It had a slow parabolic action right down to the cork," he says. "It was charismatic."

Fernandez fled with his family to the United States when Castro took power in 1959. He became an accountant, rising to budget director for the Burger King Corporation. "I hated all of it," he says. "Around 1975 I gave it all up and became an outdoor writer and photographer. "I've never looked back."

Today, Fernandez gives slide shows, consults for outdoor suppliers and boat makers, writes and photographs for magazines, and fishes all over the world. Of course, he knows more about bonefish than he did in 1968, and more about this fly.

"I suspect that fly, when moved a little quickly, imitates the snapper rather than a crustacean," Fernandez says. "I originally tied it with a kiptail wing, later with bucktail and artificial hair. The wing type depends on what you want the fly to do. Artificial hair and kiptail sink faster than bucktail. The bucktail is bulkier. It pushes more water."

The Special is tied in hook sizes Nos. 2 to 8. Fernandez goes as small as a No. 6 in areas like the Bahamas, where there are large schools of small bonefish. When the fish are cruising in the deeper water, he throws a No. 2, as he does in the Keys. The classic and most common size for a bonefish fly is a No. 4.

Fernandez works the bright, shiny Special a little faster than he would a dark fly. But fast is a relative term, Fernandez says. Bonefish, unlike barracuda, don't chase fast fish.

Contrary to popular perception, bonefish are not that fast, Fernandez says. "There are faster fish," he says. "Many fish with a tight wrist tail are faster: barracuda, kingfish, wahoo. But the bonefish is great because it can run for distance. The 'cudas are like cheetahs. Thirty yards and they're through."

Bonefish Special

Bob Rodgers estimates there are at least 200 professional fishing guides in the Florida Keys, but very few who make their living stalking the "big three"—tarpon, bonefish, and permit. He does.

"I seldom get called to guide for redfish and snook," says the 43-year-old Fishstalkers Guide Service captain.

He tailors his Buchanan Special for a very special place and time. From May to June, when water temperatures in the Keys top 80 degrees, bait pours through the shallows and shoals from Key Largo to Key West. Tarpon shadow the bait, in packs that can reach 200 fish. Rodgers says he can often see them approach from 400 or 500 yards away.

"Bayside, all you see is a changing color of water. My clients think I'm crazy when I tell them it's tarpon. When the fish take their time, moving slow, high in the water, that's when you know they're going to eat. It's like a cloud coming over the water."

Standing on the poling platform of an 18-foot Hewes Bonefisher, Rodgers waits for that apparition in a particular spot he's staked out on Buchanan Bank. After moseying across a lake, the tarpon hit the Bank, the lip of which is only a foot below the surface. Too big to cross, the tarpon end up sidling directly alongside it, and Rodgers says he can predict within a few feet where the 50- to 150-pound fish will pass. That allows him to drop his fly directly in their path ("Your best shot with a tarpon is head on," he says). The boat that picks a spot that's not a spot will catch nothing. Likewise, anglers who break out spinning tackle. "God help you," Rodgers says. "It is and always has been a fly fishing spot."

Etiquette among guides, which governs how boats come and go and where they set, is complex, to say the least. In a Thomas McGuane novel set in Key West, a novice guide poaches what an established guide perceives as his territory; the book ends in violence.

"You can't just put your boat anywhere," Rodgers acknowledges. "I've read *92 in the Shade*, and while parts of it may have been exaggerated, there have been incidents of fights and boat sinkings. There's a certain way to enter and leave and not affect anyone's fishing, and that's what keeps your boat afloat, if you know what I mean. It's cutthroat to the max."

The fly Rodgers ties to beat his competition is surprisingly small. "I found that the smaller I went, the less likely I was to spook the fish," he says, recounting the Buchanan Special's evolution. "Even if the lead fish veered away, you'd still have a shot at another fish further down the line."

Rodgers's experiments with color taught him that the chocolate and tangerine hackles inspire more tarpon to bite. But regardless of color, he hones his hooks razor-sharp for tarpon.

"The inside of a tarpon's mouth has the consistency and hardness of a cinder block," he says. "I tell my customers when they set the hook to try and kill the fish, yank the rod till it's almost breaking. Keep setting on him 10 or 15 times—then you have a chance." Even so, only one of every five or six tarpon hooked is landed. An 80- or 90-pound tarpon can drag a boat for miles.

"You never whip a tarpon," Rodgers says. "You might fight them to a draw. But you never whip them."

Buchanan Special

Tim Borski's Chernobyl Crab is custom-made for winter-migrating bonefish in the northern Florida Keys.

"Sometimes after the cold fronts blow through in winter, it's the only game in town," says the 34-year-old Borski, who can watch bonefish tailing from his kitchen window on Craig Key, a speck of an island 10 miles south of Islamorada. The key is surrounded by flats and sandwiched between the Channel 2 and Channel 5 bridges, famous among anglers.

The migrating bonefish may be the only game in the winter water, but few fly fishermen before Borski had much luck slowing the schools of up to 300 fish as they made their annual southern sprint, on the ocean side of the Keys, from Elliot Key to Key Largo. "The fish were migrating, moving quickly on the surface," Borski says. "They were off their feed. People were throwing Crazy Charlies at them, which would sink to the bottom. The bonefish would go right by."

So, in 1992, Borski developed the tempting, floating paunch of the Chernobyl. The fly swims hook side up, has lead eyes, two grizzly back hackles, a spun deer-hair body clipped semi-round, and a wide palmered hackle, bottom-trimmed. The deer-hair body elevates the fly in the water column to the sight line of the migrating bonefish, who swim in six to 10 feet of water. Borski originally named the fly the Chernobyl Hairhead because of its devastating effectiveness, but it imitated so well the crabs upon which the bonefish feed that he changed the name.

Borski, a wildlife artist, had grown up spin-casting for muskie and smallmouth bass in Wisconsin. He wasn't a fly fisher. But he'd read enough about bonefish—how "scarce, wary, and spooky they were"—that in his early twenties he traveled to the Keys, hired a guide, and broke out his spinning rod.

"Nothing I'd read prepared me for the experience," Borski says. "I couldn't believe a six-pound fish could fight harder than a muskie. My first fish nearly dumped my reel. He ran 200 yards."

Borski promptly moved to Miami and proceeded to catch as many bonefish as he could, chumming them and taking them by droves on spinning tackle. Then a thought occurred him. He wanted to take one on a fly rod—just to see what it felt like.

"That was the beginning of the whole downward spiral," he laments. Borski soon bought a cheap fly fishing outfit and hit the flats. It took him three months of hard fishing to finally pull in that first bone on a fly. "Once I caught the first one, I said I want to do this again," he says.

At the time, Borski was working in an arts and crafts store, but he started tying soon after his first success with the fly rod, eventually taking a job as a commerical tier in Islamorada—a job, he says, that gave him plenty of time to "diddle" on different patterns.

Borski has never been much of a commercial tier. "I had no discipline," he says. "If you want to make any money in commercial tying you have to tie smartly and quickly. I was always fooling around, experimenting."

Borski doesn't tie commercially anymore. But he's left the legacy of Chernobyl for future generations of fly rodders, so they'll stand a chance when the big schools of bonefish head south, past Borski's kitchen window.

Chernobyl Crab

"There's nothing like exploring virgin water," says **Mike Wolverton**. "I was lucky enough to be involved in exploring Los Roques—a group of islands off the coast of Venezuela—in the late 1980s. We were the first non-native sports fishermen to successfully fish these waters."

Roques islanders had fished the water for centuries. But not for bonefish, not on fly tackle, and certainly not with the deadly Flats Master, an orange marabou confection with a tan Craft Fur wing that Wolverton had developed several years earlier.

Ed Rice, the owner of the International Sportsman's Expositions, organized the expedition to Los Roques. Rice had been fishing for sailfish and white marlin off La Guaira, 35 miles outside Caracas, when he heard about the offshore islands—virgin flats rippling with tailing bonefish.

For the exploratory trip Rice assembled eight anglers. The first thing Wolverton noticed as they approached the islands were the gorgeous, pristine white sand flats backed by mangroves and dotted with huts and huge stacks of conch shells.

Though it looked like an ideal bonefish environment, the group didn't find fish in numbers—until Wolverton suggested they explore a distant flat he had seen from the tower of one of the boats. He and Ray Beadle took off in a small skiff. When they hit the flat, Wolverton spotted tailing bonefish. He leaped from the boat, cast, and hooked a fish before Beadle even had a chance to disembark.

"Bonefish heaven" is how Wolverton remembers the experience. "There were squadrons of fish," he says. "Everyone caught them. A lot of fish were taken on Flats Masters. We caught enough fish over five pounds to feel comfortable there were even larger fish to be found. "

The Rice group fished Los Roques for three days. When word got out about their exploits, crowds followed. But Venezuela was reluctant to open the unspoiled islands to sports fishing, and the fishery itself was problematic. A couple of lodges that opened on the islands have failed.

Anglers assumed that because the islands are near the equator, the fishing would be good year-round. Not so. "Our fishing frontiers are diminishing rapidly," Wolverton says. "Especially with the current boom saltwater fly fishing is experiencing. It's tough to find any 'new' water, and I love the unknown. It's part of all of us. There are not many new vistas left. But, even so, I will never tire of revisiting the old ones."

Raised in southern California, Wolverton, now in his early 50s, grew up fishing, surfing, and swimming in the ocean. As a young man, he moved to a farming/ranching operation outside Twin Falls, Idaho. He consults for tackle manufacturers and fishing lodges and works as a contributing editor for two fly fishing magazines.

When Wolverton created the Flats Master, it combined several existing patterns with his knowledge of food naturally available on the flats. He has expanded the fly's color variations to include white, pink, fluorescent chartreuse, orange, and yellow. He likes to attach the fly to the leader with a loop knot so the fly can hinge and "swim."

Flats Master

Steve Huff, who is known as one of the best, if not the best working saltwater fly rod guide, was drawn to the Florida Everglades by what that unusual ecosystem didn't have.

"You can ride for five hours and not see anything made by man," says Huff. "The Everglades are a totally pristine environment—just like God made it."

While Huff, 50, has not forsaken the busier waters of the Florida Keys, where he cut his teeth in the early 1970s, he's spending an increasing amount of time in the Everglades. He's building a house in Everglades City, a place he describes as a "little town in a swamp," and he swings back and forth between Ten Thousand Islands, along the southwest coast of Florida, and Duck Key.

In the Everglades, Huff pursues an eclectic mix of fish, but his favorite is snook—because of where they live, how they strike, and how they fight. "They are a classy fish," he says. "They are sneaky; they are not obvious. They slink around. There is something sinister about them.

"You've done something when you catch one; it's not easy. I don't like it to be easy. I like it to be tough," Huff says. He describes the snook's strike as "extremely explosive. Aggressive. A snook could just come over and take the fly. But they maul it. They crash it. They try and kill it. When they strike it's like a cherry bomb going off. It's fun and scary."

Huff developed Hot Lips to sate his snook passion. The fly's materials are nothing special. "It's made from chicken feathers and sheet foam," says Huff. "But it works."

Hot Lips is a top-water fly. Fish it slow, Huff advises. As the snook accelerates, plunk the fly a few times, stand back, get ready, and watch out.

Huff, born in Miami, started guiding shortly after graduating from the University of Miami in 1968 with a degree in marine biology. He thought he'd try it for a few years. "I'm still trying it," he says.

As a kid, Huff had read about the famous guides of the day in popular sporting magazines like *Field & Stream*, *Outdoor Life*, and *Sports Afield*. He religiously followed a column in the *Miami Herald* on fishing, guides, and the Keys. "The guides of that time," says Huff, "were like Mickey Mantle to me. Stu Apte, Jimmy Abright. I eventually got to know them."

Now Huff himself stands above most of the field. "He's certainly one of the best guides in the Keys," testifies author and veteran saltwater fly fisherman Tom Ernhardt. "He's on anybody's top-five list. He fishes 270 days a year. He can teach casting, fly tying, knots. He knows all the species he goes after—their habitat and requirements. He works hard and he's extraordinarily bright."

When Huff started out, the fishing in the Keys was nothing short of spectacular, he says. He'd go for whole days without seeing another boat. There was never anyone cluttering his favorite flats.

Those days are gone: The Keys have become a circus. And even the Everglades are being discovered, he says, "like everywhere else in the world."

Hot Lips

There's nothing subtle in **Jeffrey Cardenas**'s presentation of his Marquesa Sunrise Special to tarpon.

"I like to throw the Sunrise close to fish, right in front of their nose, usually within 18 inches," says Cardenas, owner of Key West's Saltwater Angler, a specialty fly fishing outfitter. "I alter the standard six-inch tarpon strips to a jerkier retrieve if the tarpon doesn't take the fly."

The Sunrise's orange color approximates shrimp native to the Marquesas—a group of islands 24 miles due west of Key West, where Cardenas, now in his early 40s, guided for many years.

The Marquesas are a special place for Cardenas, wild islands situated on the seam between two great bodies of water—the Gulf of Mexico and the Atlantic Ocean. The tremendous tidal flow between the Ocean and the Gulf brings enormous amounts of bait, which in turn attract predators like the barracuda, shark, and tarpon.

Cardenas fished the Sunrise when he took his houseboat, the *Huck Finn*, to the Marquesas in August 1994. The six weeks he spent there in splendid isolation—loafing, exploring, and fishing—provided the material for his beautiful book, *Marquesa*, illustrated by A. D. Tinkham.

Bill Trego, the book's publisher, describes *Marquesa*'s inception: "Very early in the morning he came in and said 'Get up.' We ran out to the Marquesas and watched the sunrise. It was the most thrilling, sublime morning I'd spent in years. We listened to birds squealing and squawking for hours. I had a definite idea of the book I wanted Jeffrey to write. He had a very different book in mind. He wrote his book. It's Huck Finn goes to Walden Pond in the Florida Keys."

In one particularly memorable scene in *Marquesa*, Cardenas awakens in the predawn, tarpon bumping against the *Huck Finn*'s hull. He climbs to the boat's roof, casting to tarpon in the dark, a practice Key West guides call "splooshing."

It is the kind of solitary poetic event that often unfolds for Cardenas in *Marquesa*. "It doesn't take many strikes before I work myself up into the frenzy of a splooshing tarpon," Cardenas writes. "I hoot and holler, scrabbling for balance as my toes come precariously close to the edge of the roof.... The lagoon is aglow with phosphorescence."

Dawn brightens the sky and the tarpon come off their feed, languidly like a daisy chain. This is the time for the Sunrise Special. The fly's orange and tan marabou are vivid against the water's turtlegrass bottom.

Cardenas ties the Sunrise with a 2/0 hook for easy penetration. Like many tiers, he uses marabou in the fly's tail for lifelike action. When it hits the water, the tail is usually the first thing the tarpon sees. "When the fly is stripped, it undulates." Cardenas says. "Although it doesn't look like a shrimp in appearance, it does in its profile and movement."

Cardenas, who grew up in Plantation, Florida, was raised along the water and settled in Key West 15 years ago.

He didn't turn to guiding simply because he liked to fish. "Guiding," he says, "allowed me more of an opportunity to spend time in an environment that I had grown up with and learned to love."

Marquesa Sunrise Special

Gulf of Mexico

From the vast, steaming inland of the Florida Everglades, to the famed grassy flats of Texas, the hard-fighting redfish and wily sea trout are the main quarry of Gulf fly casters. Hot spots that produce massive numbers of fish include the Everglades' Ten Thousand Islands, the balmy channels and bays backing the Gulf Islands National Seashore between Destin and Pensacola, the brackish "gumbo" mud flats of Louisiana, and the scores of unspoiled saltwater lakes tracing the Texas coastline from Galveston to Brownsville.

From June through August, temperatures on the Texas flats hover in the 90s; it's humid, with constant wind. This is the time of year the sea trout venture inland, where they're stalked in glassy water six inches to five feet deep, with deeper potholes. The prime times for redfish on the flats are summer and fall, when temperatures drop into the 80s. In the Everglades, spring and fall produce the best head of fish; water temperatures drop into the 60s during the winter, and in summer the glades are swamped by fresh water from storms.

Tested fly patterns in the Gulf include the ubiquitous shrimp—in a dizzying array of sizes, colors, and ties; large mullet patterns for trophy trout; and mud minnows with weed guards.

MISSISSIPPI
ALABAMA
TEXAS
LOUISIANA
GEORGIA
FLORIDA
GULF OF MEXICO

It is a happy state of affairs for **Brooks Bouldin** that when the water temperature drops and the redfish vanish from Gulf of Mexico barrier islands like San Jose and Mustang, speckled trout move in, lurking in the deepest channels and ambushing bait as it is swept off the flats with the tide.

Bouldin, owner of the Angler's Edge fly tackle shop in Houston, pursues them with his Brooks's Shrimp. He ties the Shrimp with a long-shank stainless-steel hook, a Seal-ex dubbed body, and a carapace of Swiss straw. The grizzly hackle and horsehair tentacles give the fly its long silhouette.

When tracking speckled trout, the largest of which run 28 or 30 inches, Bouldin throws the Brooks's because he wants his fly to get down into the pot holes where the fish settle. (Clouser Minnows and Zonkers, he says, are also deadly against trout in the pots.)

Bouldin describes the potholes as sandy-bottomed areas that range from the size of a bathtub to the size of a living room. For miles along the shoreline the water will be ankle- to waist-deep, an endless sea of salt grass and shallows. Then the potholes open up, six inches deeper than what surrounds them. Bouldin drags the Shrimp across a hole and the speckled trout spring.

Bouldin, now in his mid-fifties, grew up in Houston, a city his Georgia-bred grandfather rode to on horseback 100 years ago. He's had his shop since the mid-1980s. "My banker and I own it," he chuckles caustically. Before he ran the shop, he was in real estate.

Bouldin tied his first fly when he was 15, from chenille and bucktail. "It was an awful mess," he recalls. But he took it to Yellowstone and caught cutthroat. "Something clicked," he says. He started seriously tying flies in the early 1970s and helped found the Houston Fly Fishing Club, a group which now claims about 200 members.

Bouldin says sight-casting the back barrier salt lakes in a kayak reflects the essence of what appeals to him about fly fishing. "The fly rod is something for me to stalk fish with like a bow hunter," he says. "It's about stealth, serenity, simplicity, a closeness to nature. The kayak complements the fly rod. I feel a part of what's going on. The islands work on island time. And with the kayak and fly rod, I blend into that tempo."

Brooks's Shrimp

On the salt grass flats of the Gulf barrier islands three hours south of Houston, **Brooks Bouldin** needed a shrimp pattern for redfish that wouldn't drop too quickly through water just six inches deep. His trusty Brooks's Shrimp sank too fast. It was in the grass before the redfish had a chance to see the fly and move in for the kill.

"The redfish sometimes get back into the shallow water where their backs and dorsal fins are exposed," says Bouldin. "They do get sunburned," he adds in his slow Texas drawl. "They come in from the Gulf silver, but when they've been back awhile they become copper-colored. They don't become irritable with the sunburn. They just get hungry."

Bouldin sight-casts his floating Caribou Shrimp to reds he sees rolling and rooting, their coppery backs glinting in the sun. The Caribou is full-bodied, with pearl Krystal flash tentacles, a calf tail, a caribou horn and two large nymph eyes. Its spade shape is spun caribou with badger hackle palmered through it, trimmed on the top. Bouldin dresses the Caribou just as he would a bass bug, floating it on the surface of the lakes.

The barrier islands are low and narrow, mostly shallow dunes spiked with grass, scrub, and cactus. To get to them, Bouldin launches a 14-foot sea kayak from Rockport and paddles across the inland channel. He noses his way into the outback lakes through shallow, narrow waterways cut by the tides.

Bouldin says the kayaks are so quiet that he spooks fish right under the boat, but the reds often move off only 20 or 25 feet. So Bouldin backs off, drops anchor, steps from the boat, and starts casting.

The kayak fisherman's nemesis in these shallow lakes are motorized sleds that look like wide skis or toboggans. Their draft is so shallow they can almost travel on wet ground, says Bouldin. They cut up the grass and the things that live in it. But when they aren't around, barrier fishing is a tranquil experience. When fishing with a buddy, Bouldin wears a voice-activated radio headphone so he can share his friend's fishing foibles blow by blow, even when they're fishing a fair distance apart.

The redfish are in the barrier islands most of the year, any time the water temperature tops 70 degrees. Even on a warm, sunny day between January and March, the flats' water temperature will shoot up, and suddenly the reds return, resuming their forage.

Redfish caught in the barrier back country run to 32 inches, Bouldin says. At 40 inches, they generally stay out in the Gulf. Bouldin stalks them with a 6- to 8-weight rod, depending on the wind. He uses an 8-weight floating line, a tapered leader, and a tippet with 10- to 15-pound test.

The flats environment appears sterile to the naked eye, Bouldin says, but appearances are deceiving. Once, with a home-made seine, he scooped up heaps of widgeon grass and couldn't believe the lushness of the life lying just beneath the surface.

"There were shrimp from three-quarters to three inches long," he says. "Dozens and dozens and dozens of them. There were eels as long as my index finger. There were scores of tiny crabs and fin fish. We don't see it. But those redfish do."

Caribou Shrimp

Retirement has given former jeweler **Corbett A. Davis, Sr.**, plenty of time to apply his mastery of the miniature to fly-tying innovations. "I have nothing to do with my fingers but play," says the 67-year-old creator of the infamous Crustacean A.D., so named by its maker because he considers it "the best shrimp bait since the year of our Lord."

Davis's life-like Crustacean is a deadly confection of fox squirrel tail, chenille, pearlescent tubing, and 30-pound extra-stiff, black monofilament for antenna. Davis likes to fish it at night from his favorite spot—a 240-foot private pier stretching into Pensacola Bay at the western tip of the Florida Panhandle, a stone's throw from the Alabama border. At the lip of the pier, a powerful halogen light, mounted on a pole, beams into the water. "It's like an aquarium," Davis says. "Fish swarming all over the place."

In summer, when the water is warm and the wind blows from the north with an outgoing tide, Davis cleans up, throwing a long sinking line 60 or 70 feet into the light chop. The Crustacean hooks countless speckled trout, white trout, redfish, and pinfish (Sailor's Choice). Many of his fish are relatively small. But fishing the pier for Davis is a ritual; from his familiar but dramatic spot he can watch the nuances of how the fish move and feed.

In the Gulf proper and the Florida Keys, the Crustacean has caught bonefish, cobia, snook, Spanish mackerel, bonito, mangrove snapper, and small barracuda, according to Corbett, Jr., Davis's son, who took over the family's jewelry store and is an avid saltwater fly fisher himself. "He ties 'em, I steal 'em and fish with them," the younger Davis jokes. "He puts more into his flies than anyone I've ever seen. He'll spend hours on one fly just to get it right. He's precise and conscious of detail. He's got the dexterity and patience."

Corbett, Sr., watched shrimp swimming for hours in an aquarium before building the Crustacean. He's also studied how they move when pursued by large fish in the Keys. "With big fish the shrimp come up to the top," says Davis. "When they're in danger they flick backwards. They can walk on the bottom with their five front legs and then flick right out of the water when a fish comes after them. I tie them red-brown for redfish and green and white for the speckled trout."

Davis suggests experimenting with fishing the Crustacean. First, throw it and let it sink to the bottom. Then bring it back with slow strips. If that's not working, strip it as fast as you can with two hands. Or try just letting it sit on the bottom.

President of the Gulf Coast Fly Fishers club, Davis has been fishing the Gulf for 45 years, fly fishing it for 10. The speckled trout of Pensacola Bay seem to hold a special fascination for him. Hooked, they make one or two leaps, he says, then a fast run. They may not fight as hard as redfish, but, Davis says, "you have to baby the big fish bringing them in because of their weak mouths. I lose a lot."

Perhaps the most endearing thing about the specks is their fondness for the artificials Davis ties up for them. "They like the Crustacean a lot," he says. "When the mood takes them, they'll snap it up just as fast as I can cast."

Crustacean A.D.

Before **Carl Hanson**'s grandfather died in Rockport, Massachusetts, in 1918, he taught his four-year-old grandson to snell lines, a skill Carl would use some 25 years later to create the venerable Glass Minnow. Nearly eight decades later, Hanson still puts that fly through its paces in the turtlegrass flats of Florida's Fort DeSoto Park, just south of St. Petersburg. "I'll be 82 next month. If I live that long," Hanson says.

"It's one of the best parks in the world," Hanson says of DeSoto. "And some of the best wading. There's enough wading there for 25 lifetimes."

Hanson, who has lived in St. Pete since 1950, gets up many days at 5 and is out in the turtlegrass by 7. He's especially enraptured by the ladyfish that swerve enticingly through the shallows, preying on silverside and shrimp. The fish come to Hanson as he stands knee-deep in the shallows of his favorite spot—Bunces Pass.

"The tide comes in, the fish come in. The tide goes out, the fish go out," he says. "I fish with barbless hooks. Throw them all back. I try not to hurt them."

Hanson snares about two dozen ladies each morning. They aren't big fish, growing only to 18 inches and a pound-and-a-half, and they're so full of bones that they're nearly inedible. But after a lifetime of casting flies in salt, they're Hanson's fish of choice.

"They make 25 or 30 jumps," he says. "They're an amazing fish on light tackle. They take the fly, kapow! Then they're gone. Off and running."

Hanson pursues the ladies with a five-foot, 1-weight split bamboo rod made by Jon Clarke, and a tippet tied of his wife's hip-length hair—now silvery gray instead of its once deep black. "Her hair makes the perfect tippet," he says. "I've caught fish to three-and-a-half pounds on it. She thinks I'm crazy. But what do I care?"

Hanson's wife, his second, was his first wife's best friend. Three years after he was widowed, they were married in a ceremony under crossed fly rods. She, too, fly fishes. "You should see the line she throws," says Hanson, whistling. "Real pretty! She's good."

Aside from ladyfish, Hanson takes sea trout, needlefish, redfish, and tarpon on the Minnow. The fly is tied with bucktail and monofilament snelled over foil, with a double wing that's green and brown.

"I've caught thousands of fish on them," says Hanson. "I've also put a cork on the front and fished them in fresh water for bass."

Hanson hosts a free fly-tying workshop in his living room once a week. As many as 30 people show up. He practices casting on his lawn several times a week. "I can make a fly rod dance," he says. "I can hit a tennis ball every time at 30 feet with a fly."

He's practiced long enough. In Rockport, he grew up casting the Minnow in salt water. Traditional surf casters, of course, thought he was out of his mind. "They thought I was a nut!" he says, sounding a familiar refrain. "What did I care?"

"I stopped going to church at 15, but I'm a religious man," he explains. "And my religion is simply this: Hurt as few people as you can. Help anybody. Enjoy life. Love people."

And if you love the ladyfish, let them go.

Glass Minnow

In New Orleans's backyard, **Kirk Dietrich** poles through the shallow estuaries of the Mississippi, 100 miles from where the river enters the Gulf of Mexico. When he spots a tailing redfish he ties on his Rattle Rouser, a bucktail-winged, mylar-bodied baitfish imitation whose body is stuffed with a BB-filled, plastic capsule that rattles enticingly when the fly is stripped through the brackish water.

"You should lead the fish with the fly in the same way you lead a duck or quail on the wing in bird hunting," Dietrich instructs. "It's essential when fishing the rattler to retrieve in short even strips to get the BBs rattling in the fly's casing."

Dietrich, a cartographic technician with the Army Corps of Engineers, came up with the idea for the Rattle Rouser when his friend Tom Jindra told him about John Cave's rattling flies and asked if Dietrich could design some patterns targeted for the species and conditions in the central and western Gulf of Mexico. Dietrich said that initially the Rattle Rouser took off in Texas for stalking redfish on the flats, but these days it's also popular in southern Louisiana, where fly fishing in salt water is "soaring."

Redfish aside, the Rouser is also a potent weapon against sea trout and bass. Dietrich says tying the lustrous, colorful fly is easy: "Slip the capsule inside the mylar and cinch the mylar down. There's your body quick and easy. Epoxy over mylar. To make it more durable, saturate the area with super glue before epoxying the mylar."

Dietrich's favorite type of fishing is by sight, in six inches to two feet of water. He ties the Rouser on an inverted hook to keep it free of obstructions, mud, and grass. The "gumbo" bottom of the marshes Dietrich frequents, while not quite quicksand, is super-soft and sulfur-rich.

"You put your foot in there and it's like opening a box of kitchen matches and inhaling," he says. "It's toxic."

The redfish, on the other hand, like the mud well enough; it teems with a rich array of feed—snails, shrimp, crab, and minnows. The redfish grub the gumbo for food and get fat fast. Dietrich says the fish he catches are three to five years old, generally weighing in at eight to 10 pounds. A 12-pound fish in the marshes is considered large.

Mature redfish spawn in the passes that lead from the inland estuaries to the Gulf. Females shoot eggs and males shoot sperm into the incoming tide. The fertilized eggs drift inland and settle in the adjoining bays. The young redfish live there for a short period and then travel to the interior marshes within their first year of life They thrive in the marsh's relatively benign environment before venturing out to join the spawning schools of big fish in the deep water of the Gulf. "It's a dynamic water system," says Dietrich. "Shallow bayous, bays, lakes, and ponds."

On his 8- or 9-weight rod and forward-weighted line, Dietrich uses a 12- to 15-pound tippet. Dietrich prefers a hefty rod to punch through winds often whipping at a stiff 10 or 15 knots. He ties on the heavy tippet because he dislikes losing fish, and, in summer, when the warm water lacks oxygen, light leaders lead to long, exhausting fights that kill fish.

"But I don't horse them in on the 12-pound," says Dietrich. "You can't do that to a redfish anyway."

Kirk's Rattle Rouser

The first time **Jim Stewart** tied his Snook-a-roo, his 26-year-old son grabbed it fresh off the vice, ran four blocks to the Tampa Yacht Club, waded into the balmy waters of Hillsboro Bay, cast, and landed a 28-pound snook.

"I think you've got a winner, Dad!" Stewart remembers his son yelling as he ran back to the house.

Since that fateful day in the early 1990s, Stewart's exotic red, white, and blue fly of grizzly and marabou has nailed many a snook and a variety of other fish—Stewart has also caught tarpon, redfish, sea trout, and cobia on the fly in salt water, and in fresh, bass and muskie.

The Snook-a-roo features an anal spot, which Stewart says he introduced to fly tying. The marabou simulates gills. "I like gills for snook," he says.

Stewart fishes for snook with a 9-foot, 9-weight Sage IMX Rod. He likes a stiff rod for salt water since the flies he ties have a high wind resistance. The heavier rod is as much to move the fly as it is to move the fish.

"Fishing for snook is like fishing for largemouth bass," he says. "You're looking for underwater structures. Snook have a tendency to feed on the incoming tide. They can feed furiously like bass, but they have more strength and longevity. They run far and leap from the water."

One memorable leaping snook Stewart hooked catapulted from the water of the Florida Everglades' Ten Thousand Islands and landed a foot and half up in the mangroves.

Stewart, 59, ran his own architectural firm in Tampa before selling it a few years ago. He says that fly tying is like architecture because it demands that he design for a specific purpose.

Stewart's flies have been praised for their beautiful color and full-bodied shape. He designed the Snook-a-roo to move over the water erratically and make a surface commotion when snook detonate on top like bass, but to dive when appropriate. The fly can also be fished underwater when the snook are furtive and moody, skulking in the murky shadows of the mangroves. It can be dived deep and once down fished slowly.

Stewart says he fishes at night, but always by boat, since snook territory harbors rays. Even when using the Snook-a-roo by day, Stewart wades carefully, sloshing his feet along the bottom to dislodge the docile rays, which shoot from their camouflaged beds, streaming away when disturbed.

Fly fishing first possessed Stewart when he was 13, growing up in rural Tennessee. His father taught him to cast and tie flies and they fished for bass and bluegills. Stewart moved to Florida in 1964 but didn't begin fly fishing in salt water until the mid-1980s. He structured his flies to imitate his favorite casting plugs.

Stewart is still an avid bass man as well as a snook aficionado, but bass brood on the bottom when the water turns cold, so during the winter months Stewart finds himself in salt water.

"To tell you the truth," he confesses, resignation and guilty pleasure in his voice, "I don't care whether I'm fishing fresh or salt, or what I'm fishing for—as long as I'm out there."

Snook-a-roo

Pacific

From the teeming salmon fishery of Bristol Bay in Alaska to the famed billfish banks off Costa Rica and Panama, the Pacific coast spans an astonishing range of fly-rod sport. A plethora of exotic species inhabit the blue water off the Baja coast. Sea-run salmon and cutthroat are targeted in the cooler waters off British Columbia, Washington, and Oregon. Inshore, anglers plumb Puget Sound for coho and chinook salmon, while murky San Francisco Bay yields a healthy head of striped bass.

In the Northwest, a new species for the fly rod is halibut, a bottom feeder that grows to an enormous size. Angler Mark Mandell likens peeling halibut off the bottom to raising a lead garbage can top.

Angler Dan Blanton says that from California south the opportunities for inshore and near-shore fly rodders have increased during the last two decades due to the banning of gill nets and environmental cleanup efforts.

"The kelp bass have come back," says Blanton. "The salmon have come back in Monterey Bay. There's fishing for bonito and yellowtail near shore and inshore. You can catch blue sharks, and the mako shark fishing can be excellent in the high summer."

In Baja, the Mexican government is protecting its sport-fishing resource to a greater extent than in the past, though there's still room for improvement, Blanton says.

PACIFIC OCEAN
WASHINGTON
MONTANA
OREGON
IDAHO
NEVADA
UTAH
CALIFORNIA
ARIZONA

The 100-pound sailfish "ate" the Big Game Tube Fly eight times before **Cam Sigler**, the fly's creator, was finally able to hook him. Sigler had been fishing out of Tropic Star Lodge in Pinas Bay, Panama. "That lodge has released more billfish than anywhere else in the world," he reminisces fondly. "The first day we were there we watched a boat go north. It came back with 26 sailfish flags flying! We followed suit the next day."

Sigler says he and a friend hooked 41 sailfish and caught 26 during that trip on Sigler's gaudily colored, 10- to 12-inch tube flies. Four times they had doubles on, simultaneously fighting leaping sailfish.

The Tropic Star is one of Sigler's favorite haunts. Rivers pour off jungle-cloaked mountains that cut into the Pacific. "It's an incredibly rich environment," Sigler says. "There are just an amazing number of fish...and no mosquitoes!" He sighs.

Sigler, who lives in Vashon, Washington, owns a company that designs flies and other outdoor products. He goes to Pinas to find sailfish in April and May and goes back in mid-winter for black marlin. He also fishes off Mexico and suggests Costa Rica and Guatemala as other great locations.

His technique for taking sailfish on a fly is to work in tandem with a friend. One partner trolls a hookless bait, usually mackerel or artificial, to "tease" the fish towards the boat. As the sailfish erupt behind the craft and streak toward the bait, the teaser is pulled toward the boat. When the fish closes, the other partner presents his mammoth flies on a short cast of perhaps 10 or 20 feet. By this time, the sailfish are so riled "they would strike your shoe if you put it out there," Sigler says. "In fact," he adds, "Mark Sosin, from Boca Raton, Florida, caught one on his cigar using this method."

Bills are not the only species taken with the Tube Fly. According to Sigler, fellow angler Teddy Lund recently caught a 38-pound redfish, a 6 lb. line record, off the central Florida coast.

Sigler's Big Game Tubes are tied in Sri Lanka and can be rigged six ways. They can be fished as sliders with the foam head facing nose forward, or as poppers with the head in the reverse position. The flies are basically two streamers tied together, an idea that came to Sigler from years of tube-fly fishing for salmon in the Northwest. But they can also be taken apart and fished separately. "I wanted a big silhouette," Sigler says of his line of hydra-headed monsters. "I like big, big oval eyes. They really turn the fish on."

Sigler and his big game cohorts use pitbull rods—eight or eight-and-a-half feet long—that dead-lift 22 pounds off the floor. His four- to six-inch diameter reels hold 600 to 800 yards of backing for marlin and 300 to 500 yards for sailfish.

"It's a challenge having an eight-foot fish jumping off the end of your fly rod," he chuckles. "I've never killed one, but I have released some gorgeous fish."

Big Game Key Lime Squid

The black marlin surfaced, overtaking the teaser that skipped and hopped in the deep blue and foaming white of Hannibal Bank, Panama. The marlin slashed at the teaser—gnawing, humping, striking—as Benito, **Winston Moore**'s guide out of Club Pacifico, jerked the hookless bait closer and closer.

"Now!" yelled Moore. The captain threw the boat into neutral, Benito yanked the teaser from the water and Moore sent his Billfish Fly sailing toward the incensed fish. The 450-pound black slammed the fly and took off, jumping more than 70 times before Moore finally brought it boat-side one-and-a-half hours later.

"I usually release every fish I land," says Moore, who started fly fishing in salt water in the late 1950s. "In this case, because it was such an accomplishment, I was going to kill the fish for the record book. But we couldn't get him into the boat. We tried putting a line around him. All we had on board was a dorado gaff."

Moore's boat radioed another nearby for a stronger gaff—but it was 20 minutes until help arrived. In the meantime, the marlin had been gathering its strength. When the other boat came alongside, the fish heaved from the water and rocketed away. Moore fought the marlin for another four hours, but it sounded, and he couldn't move it to the surface. He intentionally broke the fish off in order to get back to camp before dark.

The black is one of six marlin—two black, two striped, and two blue—that Moore has brought in on a fly rod. Now 71, he has, by all accounts, caught more Pacific sailfish on a fly—138—than anyone else.

In his billfishing days, Moore used a Seamaster reel and a J. Kennedy Fisher fiberglass blank 12/13-weight rod custom-built for heavy fish. He came up with the Billfish Fly, which he's never formally named, in the 1950s.

The foam tube on the fly's head is fished with the tapered side forward so the fly works as a slider rather than a popper. A shock tippet is run through the tube in the head. Moore uses about six color combinations: red and white; blue and white; blue, green, and white; green and yellow; all white; and orange and yellow.

Moore, who still makes his living from commercial real estate ventures in Boise, Idaho, says he doesn't remember how the fly evolved. Anyway, he adds, the shape of the fly and the materials aren't terribly important when you're fly fishing billfish. "If the fish has been teased right and you throw your tennis shoe out there, he'll take it," he says. "They get so angry. These are fish that are used to ruling the ocean. They're not used to having food taken away from them."

These days, Moore fishes for permit exclusively. He stalks the flats of Ascencion Bay on the Yucatan, and the flats of Belize south to Guatemala.

Explaining why he's forsaken all other fish, Moore says: "Permit are the ultimate challenge. They take the most finesse, cunning, patience, and skill. Of course, you have to be semi-unbalanced to fish for them. You go days without seeing one. Then when you do, the odds are against you."

Billfish Fly

On a cold, overcast, November morning just after dawn, **Les Johnson** walked through a stand of conifers to the edge of Washington's Puget Sound at Lincoln Park in Seattle. Forty feet offshore he saw several resident coho salmon rolling and jumping in the gentle chop.

Johnson, now in his early 60s and author of numerous fly fishing books, tied on his tried-and-true Johnson Sand Lance, a fly he's fished for 20 years, and cast to a coho that rolled nearby. It wasn't long before he'd caught and released a couple of fat 18-inchers.

"On my next cast the grab was really hard," says Johnson. "I thought for a moment that I might be into a small chinook salmon. Then it rolled and I knew that it was a sea-run cutthroat trout." Johnson landed the heavy-shouldered, mature sea-run—a full 20 inches long. A few casts later he hooked another cutthroat, this one 21 inches.

"I love cutthroat. They really bend the rod," Johnson says. "They fight a much more dogged battle than coho. They are bulldogs!"

Johnson should know. He wrote the book—*Fishing for Sea-Run Cutthroat Trout.* The feisty sea-run, or coastal cutthroat, indigenous to the Pacific Coast, has gorgeously black-spotted flanks. "The prettiest of trout," Johnson calls them. The sea-run lives and feeds in salt water and spawns in the fresh water of its natal stream. A trophy sea-run tops out at about 23 inches and four pounds.

The Sand Lance that Johnson cast in Lincoln Park was a smaller version of the fly pictured here. Johnson ties the Lance in sizes from one-and-a-half to five inches long. The pattern imitates the Pacific sand lance, an important bait fish for all West Coast game fish. The sand lance also lives in Atlantic coastal waters, where it is a critical bait for striped bass and bluefish. The fish is svelte and slight. It darts and shimmies, undulating over shallow, sandy bottoms, often only a few feet from shore. Johnson incorporates the slender shape of the bait fish into his fly, and it has evolved over the years to be a steady taker of salmon, sea-run cutthroat, and Dolly Varden.

"The sand lance can be fished on a floating line," Johnson says, "but I like it better on an intermediate line that doesn't get pushed around by wave action. With an intermediate that gets down just under the wave action, you are always retrieving on a tight line, making it easy to detect the light taps as well as the hard strikes."

Johnson likes tube flies. He says they last longer than traditional flies. Should the hook be damaged, you can retain the fly. The versatile tube fly can also be used with large or small hooks, singles, doubles, or trebles. Johnson's first sand lance patterns were conventional streamer imitations that evolved into tubes, then incorporated synthetic material like Super Hair when it became available. The fly took its present shape with the addition of a Bob Popovics-style epoxy head.

"Whether I'm fishing Pacific salt water near home, or on a trip, I always carry a good supply of Sand Lance tube flies," says Johnson. "It is my must-have pattern for all the salt water from Monterey Bay, California, to the Misty Fjords in southeast Alaska."

Johnson Sand Lance

When **Joe Butorac** started tying flies at age 11, he dreamed of someday making a living as a professional tier. That dream came true. Now in his early 50s, Butorac estimates he's tied over a million flies in the last four decades, the last twenty-plus years as a pro. "I've topped a million off my vice," he says. "Sometimes I say to myself, 'This is getting a little weird.' I look down at my fingers and think, 'How can they do this?' "

Butorac, who makes his home in Seattle, Washington, and has never licensed his flies, ties only his own patterns, like the Krystal Flash Tube Fly and the Flashy Lady.

The Flashy Lady mimics euphausid shrimp, which are also known as krill, small translucent creatures that swim in clouds and are a staple of the diet of whales. The krill, in contrast to most shrimp, swim head-first, eyes in front.

Butorac designed the Krystal Flash Tube Fly for adult salmon. Like the Flashy Lady, which has hooked its share of juvenile salmon, the Krystal Flash works well in the waters of the Pacific Northwest. It imitates the candlefish—a forage bait for salmon that's prevalent in Alaska in places like Craig, Prince of Wales Island, and the area around Sitka.

The Flash takes coho and chinook salmon that have come inshore and are ready to spawn. These coho run six to 20 pounds and feed in 15 to 20 feet of water. The chinooks hold deeper, though at dawn and dusk they sometimes come up to the surface to feed. The four-and-a-half-inch fly is often fished from a boat in a Baja-style troll, one angler luring a fish to surface and then the other anglers casting the other fish in the school with the fly.

"What makes this fly interesting is its iridescent coloring," says Butorac. "The underbody of bucktail gives it a fluid motion. Without it, the Krystal Flash tends to cling to itself. It doesn't have good action. The bucktail keeps it flared and much more animated in the water. The transparent thread lets the flash show through to imitate the natural's head."

The fly is usually tied with two hooks in tandem since the coho, unless they're very aggressively feeding, tend to nip at the tails of the bait. If the coho are on their feed, one front hook is sufficient. With chinook, a single hook does the trick; they nail a fly headfirst. "It's amazing that all species of Pacific salmon take a fly in completely different ways," notes Butorac.

Butorac is a rabid saltwater fly rodder. "Saltwater fly fishing was always more interesting to me than freshwater," he says. "I was always a crazed striper and salmon fisherman. "I've never tied trout flies—although I am a steelhead fanatic."

Fanatic, crazed. That might be the only way a man can explain what could prompt him to tie more than a million flies in one lifetime.

"My first fly's feathers came from my pet canaries," Butorac recalls. "At first, when the birds lost feathers I'd pick them up. But soon the birds started to lose a few feathers they didn't lose on their own."

Krystal Flash

Even to expert saltwater fly fishermen, the permit is an enigma—a fish ardently, even devoutly pursued but rarely obtained. In his classic essay, "The Longest Silence," Thomas McGuane compared trying to take a permit on a fly to baiting a tiger with a watermelon.

"Ten or 12 years ago when I first tied my Permit Fly, that was true," says **Del Brown**, 77. "We expected that out of 100 casts to permit maybe two would show interest. I tied my fly because what was out there for permit just wasn't doing the job. I never tie anything I can buy. That's my motto."

For Brown, persnickety permit are now a thing of the past. Permit may not epitomize predictability, but they can be counted on to show a healthy interest in Brown's beady-eyed, yarn-and-feather, "impressionistic" rendering of the permit's favorite food—the crab.

If the fly is given a decent cast, that is. "Of course I've beaned countless permit," Brown says.

The trick is to get the fly dropping in front of the permit. If the fly sinks to the bottom and the permit looks but doesn't take, Brown twitches and strips the line—anything to get the permit's attention and provoke a strike. These are usually futile gestures, but with permit, you never know.

"Sometimes the permit seem fascinated by the thing," says Brown. "They come up and look at it but don't take it. Then you have clutzy permits that charge the bottom, slamming their heads but missing the fly."

The Permit Fly is a hefty little morsel, and Brown casts a 10-weight rod with an 11-weight floating line. Earlier incarnations of the fly were even heavier, with hunks of glue, metal, and epoxy. They were deadly projectiles, not only for permit, but guides and anglers as well. Guide Steve Huff used to call Brown's fishing vest his "flak jacket."

Brown says one of the reasons the primitive permit flies of the past were so useless was because the old epoxy heads tended to be fished near the top. "The permit has good eyesight, and I think when it came up to look at the fly it would see the boat and bolt."

Brown ties his fly so it will head for the bottom in a quick, downward descent that mimics the defensive behavior of crabs. Brown says this movement, not appearance, is what makes the fly work.

"It's what it does, not how it looks, that is important," he insists. "Impressionism is far more important than realism."

Brown, who lives in the Monterey area of California, is on the water in the Florida Keys 100 days a year. He fishes bonefish, tarpon, and other species, but permit was long his principal passion. He holds the IGFA records for permit on 2-pound (9.75 pounds), 4-pound (24 pounds), and 8-pound test (41.5 pounds), as well as the mark for tarpon on 8-pound (127 pounds).

In addition to fishing, Brown skis 40 days a year, chaperoning high school trips. Swishing down the high Rockies, is Brown dreaming of new ways to hook permit? Not at all. "I've been fishing snook in the Everglades," Brown says, "and I've been going to Cape Cod for the past two summers for stripers. I'm devising different surface lures, working with foam flies. I'm on to new challenges."

Del's Permit Fly

"When you catch a wahoo, you feel like you've hooked a Volkswagen doing 70 miles an hour," says **Pete Parker**. "They make screaming runs for 200 or 300 hundred yards. A rooster tail shoots up from your line 18 to 20 inches."

Pete's Slider has hooked more than a few wahoo, which are thought to be the fastest fish in the ocean, reaching speeds of better than 60 miles an hour. Until recently, large wahoo have been elusive quarry on a fly rod, but Parker and his cohorts have changed all that with a technique that's brought them more and bigger fish.

Parker, who lives outside Denver, fishes the Pacific coast of Baja, Mexico, in a Lopreste-Dunn fishing yacht out of Cabo San Lucas. Twelve anglers board the Star, typically in late November or early December, and motor about 30 miles offshore.

On his first Baja trip in 1992, Parker, then in his late 50s, couldn't catch a wahoo to save his life. His Slider took every fish but—skipjack, black skipjack, bonito, yellowfin. By the end of the first day, the *Star*'s anglers had constellations on their guts from rod butts pounding into them during punishing fights for the tuna.

On that first trip, Pete's Slider captured the world record for black skipjack on a fly, 13 pounds, off Thetis Bank, Mexico. It was a hot, sunny November day with a 10-knot wind blowing from the north. Parker threw a short cast off the Star's starboard deck using a 10-weight line, 16-pound tippet, and sinking tip.

The *Star*'s sonar told him he was casting to a pod of 100 or so skipjack feeding off balls of bait. Parker threw to the school's edge. When he stripped, the Slider dove. When he paused, it rose, wiggling enticingly. The skipjack smashed the Slider from the bottom, taking off and giving Parker what he describes as "20 minutes of disbelief." "The skipjacks are just incredibly strong for their size," Parker says. "Pound for pound, they are stronger than even a tuna or wahoo."

That first trip on the *Star* was a revelation, but Parker still wanted a wahoo. On subsequent trips, he stopped using the traditional technique of double-fisted stripping as quickly as possible and began letting flies like the Slider drop on a sinking line at dead drift. On a recent trip, he and fellow anglers used that method to bring in 20 wahoo, from 36 to 66 pounds.

The wahoo often would show themselves when the boat was teasing for marlin. The mate would chum with anchovies or mackerel to bring the wahoo in, but the better casters, who could go 80 feet or more, still did better with the fish.

To fish successfully for wahoo, Parker says, you need a good reel. He recommends the Abel, Charleston, or Seamaster reels. "I've seen guys' reels just fly apart when a wahoo makes its run," he says. "Disintegrate. When that happens what comes out of their mouths is unprintable."

Parker says he's one of only two anglers he knows of who've taken a wahoo on monofilament—a 51-pound bruiser off Baja. Wahoo are always fished with a wire shock tippet since their teeth are razor sharp.

"I allowed him no rest," said Parker. "He couldn't manipulate the line in his mouth. The wind was right, the current was right. The fish gods were smiling."

Pete's Slider

Dan Blanton is one of the best-known saltwater fly-rod anglers and fly tiers in the world today. One of his claims to fame is the Whistler, a fly he created 32 years ago to look and act like a jig.

Blanton was targeting the striped bass of San Francisco Bay. "Most of the saltwater flies of that time were primitive," he says. "They were unrealistic and lacked animation."

Blanton designed the Whistler with bead eyes, a short hook and wide hackle collar, with all the weight up front, so the fly would swim and fall with a jig-like motion that fish find irresistible. He tied the Whistler with a short, red body of chenille between tail and hackle collar, imitating a bait fish's flaring gills. Blanton says these elements, combined with the broad hackle collar, helped the fly's hit rate in the turbid waters of the Bay, where three feet of visibility is considered good. The bead eyes whistled as it flew through the air, giving the fly its name.

Blanton discovered the very first run out that the Whistler "pushed the stripers' buttons," so he made only minor refinements over the years to the fly's design—sandwiching 50 or so strands of flashabou into its tail, which further animates the fly and attracts fish from a greater distance.

Some 20 versions of the Whistler circulate today. Red and white is a good all-around color scheme, as are yellow and orange, all black, and black-and-grizzly. "If I had one color for striped bass it would be black," Blanton says. "The bass love it and it works well in turbid water or darkness."

Blanton calls the Whistler "far and away one of the most productive and successful patterns ever produced. It has caught all the species you can think of, in both salt and fresh water."

Blanton, 53, grew up in California, trout-fishing the high Sierras with his father. His first fly rod was a Japanese model his dad had brought home from Japan along with a balsa-wood box of Japanese flies. He tried them out on a pond at the local golf course and has been fascinated with fly fishing ever since.

For the last 20 years, Blanton has been a writer, editor, and photographer for fly fishing magazines. Umpqua carries all his flies.

Blanton taught himself to cast and tie from books. He disassembled flies to see how they were made. He moved into saltwater fly angling when he was 15. "It was new, exciting, and different," he says. "Not many people on the West Coast were doing it."

Blanton took the Whistler with him on his first tarpon trip to Central America when he was in his early twenties. "We were the pioneers of fly fishing for tarpon in the jungle rivers of Costa Rica—the Rio Colorado and Rio Parismina," he says. "The Whistler was one of the top producers. My first time out I jumped 23 tarpon and landed 13. It's a tarpon killer at Canton Island in Honduras, and in the rivers of Venezula."

The last frontier in fly fishing, says Blanton, is blue water, far away from reefs and shores. New saltwater fisheries are also sprouting in Australia, New Guinea, Senegal, and South Africa, he says.

"There's less of an aversion to breaking with convention," Blanton says of fly fishing in salt water. "There's nothing you can't do on a fly today."

Whistler

ET TOBACCO
ELL'S
e Nuns
BACCO
E NICER"
CANADA
D24
STRIKE
"IT'S TOASTED"

United Kingdom and Denmark

Saltwater fly fishing is still in its infancy in Europe. Fly tiers mostly adapt American patterns, and because of the cold water, the variety of species available to them is limited.

Sea-run brown trout of up to 20 pounds are caught in northern Europe from the beaches of the Danish Isles and in the seaward lochs of Scotland. European sea bass that run over 10 pounds are caught in the rocky coves off Wales.

Saltwater casters also fish areas in Cornwall and Devon that hold great sandy estuaries that drain out, except for channels of water called sea pools. At the right time of year, these pools may hold salmon and sea-run brown trout that were trapped when the waters receded. Sea-run browns are also fished inshore in the Orkney Islands off Scotland. The Danish sea-run fishery draws anglers from all over northern Europe. According to Odense fly rodder Jens Staal, Danish fly fishing is growing every year, and tackle and techniques for fishing the powerful silver browns are improving all the time.

By contrast, most fly fishermen in the United Kingdom are like Britain's Robert Spaight, who views the dedication of surf and sea fishermen as a form of not-very-compelling Neanderthal heroics.

Spaight, who fishes the still-water lochs of Scotland's South Uist, says when Europeans want to fish the salt, by and large they go to the States or places like Christmas Island.

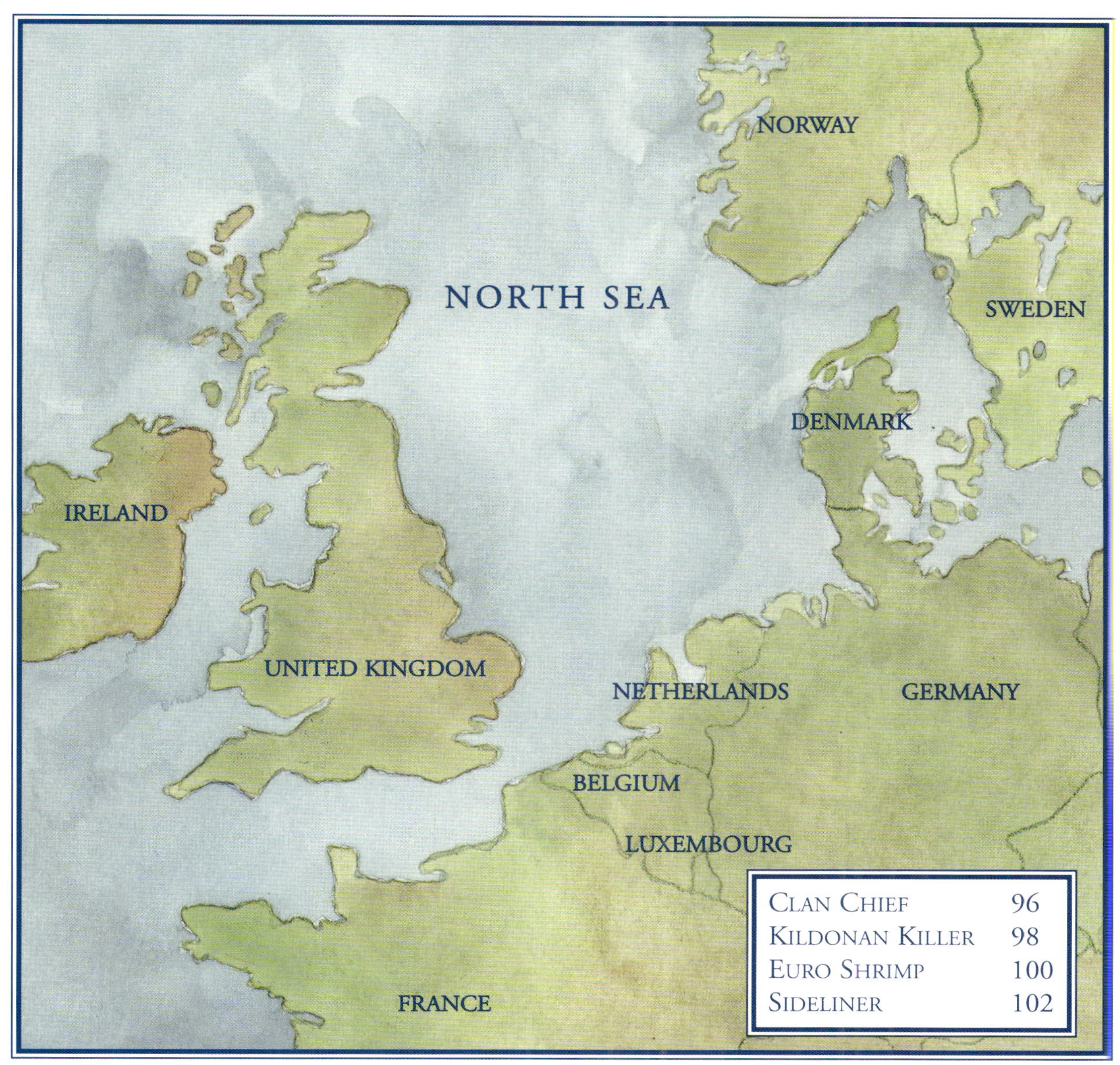
NORWAY
NORTH SEA
SWEDEN
DENMARK
IRELAND
UNITED KINGDOM
NETHERLANDS
GERMANY
BELGIUM
LUXEMBOURG
FRANCE

In the late summer and fall, the Outer Hebrides lochs of South Uist—wild, remote, and still arms of the sea 100 miles west of the Scottish port of Oban—hold sea-run brown trout that grow to 20 pounds, known as "sea trout." Uist's seaward lochs drink in huge slugs of salt water from spring tides, creating a brackish environment where **Robert Spaight** angles for the sea-runs with flies that have age-old histories.

Spaight and others have adapted these flies for the Hebrides environment. The Kildonan Killer and Clan Chief are two such adaptations. Both are tied on 14 through 6 standard-shank hooks with a combination of synthetic and natural materials. In addition to sea trout, both take Atlantic salmon that also spawn in the burns, or small streams, of the Hebrides.

Spaight, a tier, angler, and writer in his early fifties, says the Kildonan Killer is "a mongrel fly" that was created by the local gamekeeper and a visiting "gillie" (Scottish for guide).

"The Killer borrows bits from three of the flies that have proved most effective in the Uist environment," says Spaight. "It's confected of the bright blue of the Blue Zulu, contrasted with the black and silver-banded body of the Black Pennell, and the flowing ilen blue hackle (peacock neck feather) of the Goat's Toe."

Created by John Kennedy, the fishing manager of South Uist, the Clan Chief is also a hybrid. It's similar to the Irish Bumble fly, though it's smaller in construction, with a splayed profile that allows a remarkable transmission of light through its hackles in the lochs' peaty waters.

The Chief also borrows elements of the Zulu and Bibio flies, says Spaight. When it's not attracting trout or salmon, the Chief can be adapted to bottom-fish grayling. "It's a good pattern to muck about with," says Spaight.

A country minister overseeing four churches in the Benefice of Barlings parish in Lincolnshire, England, Spaight is also a solicitor, or attorney, and writes a fly fishing column for the Lincolnshire Echo. He also does BBC radio broadcasts on fly fishing and writes for national fly fishing magazines.

Spaight belongs to fly fishing organizations in both the United Kingdom and United States, and he fishes all over Europe and the U.S. But the Hebrides and their lochs hold a special place in his heart. He has thought long and hard about the lochs' sea fish, which spend two or three years in the freshwater system and then move out to sea, coming back annually to spawn. Spaight says it's a good thing no one has figured out where the sea trout go once they leave the lochs.

"They probably don't go out as far as salmon," he says. "The tragedy of the Atlantic salmon is that people figured out where they went. Then the commercial fisheries hang about and leave their nets out. But they haven't figured out where the sea trout go. I think they probably don't travel far—50 to 150 miles. They're looking for prolific sand eels. Unfortunately, modern dredging is ripping the bottom out of the sand eel habitat. Plus our continental cousins turn sand eels into oils. Both must have a detrimental effect on sea trout feeding grounds."

Still, a healthy head of sea trout appear in the

(continued on page 98)

Clan Chief

Hebrides' lochs each season. The fish position themselves in lies that they've scurried out. The gillies, often members of families that have gillied for generations, know where to find them.

Anglers fish from the lochs' banks or from small rowboats. Until recently, the Uist boats were ancient, wooden vessels, prone to leaks. Spaight says they often felt like they might disintegrate at any moment. Now some of the boats are fiberglass, but fishing from them is still an adventure.

"They can bob around like a cork in the Atlantic breezes," says Spaight. "You have nothing but the Atlantic lying off to the west, and the wind can blow up pretty fast. There's a traditional Scottish art of holding the boat in the mouth of burns that flow into the lochs. Let me tell you, it's jolly hard work."

Uist lochs are fished with a team of three flies—bob, middle dropper, and point. The flies are fished wet, with the angler "dibbling the bob fly and drawing the string back," says Spaight. Trout will hit any of the three flies.

Spaight uses a floating or intermediate line, from 5 to 8 weight. "You've got to have something to punch the wind," he says. "These are rough waters and rough fish. They're quite likely to smash you."

Spaight says the sea trout take in a "surge," like a bow wave coming towards you. "If he runs into weeds you'll probably be all right," says Spaight. "If he runs into reeds, he'll smash you. You may well spend an hour boating that fish. In a loch there's plenty of space for him to go."

Spaight started fishing the lochs of the Hebrides after a vacation there with his wife and son. The angling prospects looked good, and the following summer he brought his rods and "took it up."

The people of the Scottish islands farm small landholdings of crops and sheep. They take seasonal work, such as working as divers on North Sea oil rigs. They speak Gaelic and teach Gaelic in their schools.

"It's all light," says Spaight, explaining what captivates him about the Hebrides. "The light is as good as the south of France. It can be raining out to sea and sunny inland. It can be warm and balmy one minute and hailing the next. When the clouds come over, the whole world turns slate gray."

The people of South Uist are a God-fearing bunch, so there's no fishing Uist's lochs on Sundays. If obsessed anglers absolutely must fish on Sundays, however, there's a provision called "Sunday lochs."

These lochs are up in the hills, away from the sparse, windswept settlements of the coast. The locals go about their Sunday business, while up in the hills possessed fishermen cast and cast—out of sight, and out of mind.

Kildonan Killer

Along the Llyen Peninsula in North Wales, midsummer light lasts until 11 o'clock at night. **Gary Coxon** looks for a full tide at midnight; the last hour and a half of the tide is the best fishing, he says.

From July to September, the European sea bass he targets come to shore on late-evening incoming tides to feed on crustaceans and small bait fish. They feed in two or three feet of water.

Coxon, United Kingdom rep for the fishing equipment manufacturer Sage, says the European sea bass, which can run over 10 pounds, is cousin to the American striper. It has a dark gray back, brilliant silver sides, white belly, large mouth, and spiked dorsal fin.

"It's the best fighting sea fish we have to offer on a fly," he says. "It eats crabs, sand eels, prawns—very predatory but also a scavenger, as most predatory fish are. It's also the best eating fish there is. Absolutely superb grilled or baked with herbs."

Coxon's record with his lifelike Euro Shrimp fly is 17 bass in an evening. He fishes the fly from the rocky shoreline, casting it parallel to the waves, not into them. The fly rides the current, rolling and gliding in the swirls and swells. He uses normal trout gear, "going a bit heavier" if the wind is strong.

Now 50, Coxon has been tying trout and salmon flies since he was 15. He started tying with a big, wooden vice and horse nails to secure the hook. Business trips to the United States for Sage introduced him to saltwater fly rodding, which is in its infancy in the U.K. "It's catching on, but catching on very slowly," he says. "The fishing is absolutely superb if you don't want to catch big fish."

Coxon ties his Euro Shrimp on a 1/0 to 4/0 English bait hook. The hook's bent shank lends itself to the curved shape of the natural. It's an imitative rather than impressionistic fly—a dead ringer for the size and shape of the shrimp that lives along the Welsh coast. He cleverly uses the hinges in the bend of a drinking straw to create the shrimp's serrated body. He colors the straw with marker and then applies a coat of shiny epoxy. The effect is chitinous and amazingly lifelike. The fly's mimetic effect extends to the pheasant rump feather and crinkled nylon antenna. "Basically what I've made is the European shrimp—not the American tiger shrimp," says Coxon.

Coxon was drawn to fly fish in salt water because English rivers are "under so much pressure." He lives in Cheshire, half an hour from the polluted sea near Liverpool, but a two-hour drive from the Welsh coast he fishes.

Aside from bass, Coxon has fished in salt water with his fly rod for pollock and the small mackerel that can be caught by the bucketload along the English and Welsh coasts. "The mackerel are great fun on light tackle," he says. "But they only run to a pound, tops."

Coxon has concocted a sand eel imitation for his mackerel quests. On occasion, he's hooked small flounder with his flies. In general, however, he says, "there's not a lot out there" to be caught. The water is cold in the Celtic and North seas, and the coasts have been heavily fished for centuries. Cod and 80-pound tope lurk offshore, but no one pursues them with a fly rod.

Euro Shrimp

"During the summer months, which I call the cream of the fishing," says **Jens Staal**, "we have more success with a fly rod than on spinning tackle."

Success is a relative term. When saltwater flies began to be used in Denmark in the late 1970s and early 1980s, top anglers like Staal averaged only one sea-run brown trout a day, and daily catches today are only a bit more gratifying.

Staal throws flies like his Sideliner to the sea-runs, fish that spend two years or so in Denmark's cool murky rivers and then migrate out to the Baltic Sea, where they turn silver in color and grow to 20 pounds.

Danish saltwater anglers fish for the trout along the coast, using bait fish and shrimp imitations adapted from American patterns. Saltwater flies are popular in Denmark these days. Staal estimates that perhaps half the anglers fishing sea-runs use fly rods. These include tourists from Germany, Belgium and Holland.

Staal thinks flies work better than traditional bait because they better approximate the trout's forage of stickleback, blenny, and various species of shrimp. The richest environment for this feed is along the shore, in very shallow water, which Staal says "is extremely convenient."

Staal, 42, is co-owner of a tackle shop in Odense, the third largest city in Denmark, with a population of 160,000. Yet many days during the summer season he's out looking for trout. He's been fishing since he was a boy. "Like most kids I started out with a spinning rod and a can of worms," he says. "But I very quickly turned to fly fishing."

Staal cruises the coastal waters looking for the right conditions to nab the sea-run browns. Often, he can see them rolling and jumping on the surface. The water has to be fairly clear, with a little chop but not too much. If it's too calm, the fish spook.

Staal fishes the Sideliner under the water, retrieving it with a series of pulls and pauses. His tackle consists of a nine- or 10-foot, 7- or 8-weight rod, a floating line with shooting or weight forward head and a six-pound tippet. Staal says the relatively heavy wide-diameter tippet combats the constant Baltic winds. Without it he'd be hopelessly tangled with wind knots.

Hooked, smaller two- or three-pound browns fight aerially like rainbow trout, leaping and sprinting across the surface. As the trout increase in size, they tend to head for the bottom like freshwater browns. "Fighting the big ones can often be like walking the dog," Staal says.

Fishing for sea-run browns is good all year round, but especially good in the spring and summer months. Fish in spawning colors are illegal to keep from November 15 to January 16. The Danish government stocks a quantity of fish.

Fly rodding for sea-runs is challenging, to say the least. Staal no longer averages just a fish a day, but his best day ever brought only seven trout of varying sizes. "When I go out I don't expect to catch anything," he says. "But it's better than it used to be in the good old days. Then the fishing was harder, we didn't know what we were doing. We had it wrong."

Sideliner

Tiers Contact List

Dan Blanton
Outdoor Ventures
14720 Amberwood Lane
Morgan Hill, CA 95037
(408) 778-9133

Tim Borski
P.O. Box 122
Islamorada, FL 33036
(305) 664-9367

Brooks Bouldin
Angler's Edge
3926 Westheimer
Houstin, TX 77027
(713) 993-9981

Jaime Boyle
P.O. Box 1986
Edgartown, MA 02539
(508) 693-1995

Stephen Brettell
336 Guinea Road
Biddeford, ME 04005
(207) 283-4129

Del Brown
125 Cutter Drive
Watsonville, CA 95076
(408) 722-0725

Joe Butorac
P.O. Box 98
Arlington, WA 98223
(360) 435-8624

Jeffrey Cardenas
The Saltwater Angler
219 Simonton Street
Key West, FL 33040
(800) 223-1629

Bill Catherwood
399 Marshall Street
Tewksbury, MA 01876
(508) 851-3359

Bob Clouser
Clouser's Fly Shop
101 Ulrich Street
Middletown, PA 17057
(717) 944-6541

Gary Coxon
Dinglevale Cottage
55 Forest Road
Cuddington
Cheshire CW8 2ED, England
011-44-1606-882-891

Douglas Cummings
Royal Wulff Products
HCR 1, Box 70
Beaverkill Road
Lew Beach, NY 12758
(914) 439-4060

Corbett A. Davis, Sr.
1430 E. Bayshore Court
Gulf Breeze, FL 32561
(904) 932-3110

Kirk Dietrich
304 Chinchilla
Arabi, LA 70032
(504) 279-0523

Tom Earnhardt
2533 York Road
Raleigh, NC 27608
(919) 571-7969

Chico Fernandez
11450 SW 98th Street
Miami, FL 33176
(305) 596-4481

Ben Furimsky
BUGSKIN
615 Broadway
Rockwood, PA 15557
(814) 926-2676

Jack Gartside
10 Sachem Street
Boston, MA 02120
(617) 277-5831

Johnny Glenn
Black Fly Charters
133 Westerly Bridford Road
Westerly, RI 02891
(401) 348-8716

D.L. Goddard
8013 Shipshead Creek Drive
Easton, MD 21601
(410) 820-9762

Carl O. Hanson
217 54th Street South
St. Petersburg, FL 33707
(813) 321-4160

Bill Hayes
Angler's Pro Shop, Inc.
3361 Bethlehem Pike
Souderton, PA 18964
(215) 721-4909

Steve Huff
210 Schooner Lane
Duck Key, FL 33050
(305) 743-4361

Les Johnson
1924 E Fir Street
Seattle, WA 98122
(206) 328-3081

Bernard "Lefty" Kreh
210 Wickersham Way
Hunt Valley, MD 21030
(410) 667-4876

Winston Moore
600 North Steelhead Way
Suite 144
Boise, ID 83707
(208) 323-1919

Pete Parker
23825 San Isabel
Box 756
Indian Hills, CO 80454
(303) 697-8725

Tom Piccolo
1430 Jackson Avenue
Apt. 7
New Orleans, LA 70130
(504) 524-2768

Bob Rodgers
Fishstalkers Guide Service
P.O. Box 1510
Tavernier, FL 33070
(305) 853-0933

Cam Sigler
Cam Sigler Co.
11061 Patten Lane SW
P.O. Box 656
Vashon Island, WA 98070
(206) 567-4836

Robert Spaight
The Vicarage
Station Road
Langworth
Lincoln LN3 5BB, England
011-44-1522-754233

Jens Staal
Klaus Berntsensvej 298
DK 5260 Odense S, Denmark
011-45-65959461

Jim Stewart
1104 S. Dunbar Avenue
Tampa, FL 33629
(813) 287-2761

Lou Tabory
96 Pine Mountain Road
Ridgefield, CT 06877
(203) 798-8052

Richard Whitner
The Sporting Life
601 Julia Street
New Orleans, LA 70130
(504) 529-3597

Mike Wolverton
4955 East 2900 North
Murtaugh, ID 83344
(208) 432-6614

Mail-order Suppliers

Angler's
4955 East 2900 North
Murtaugh, ID 83344
(800) 657-8040

Angler's Covey
917 West Colorado Avenue
Colorado Springs, CO 80905
(800) 753-4746

Angler's Expressions
P.O. Box 3136
Boise, ID 83703
(800) 634-3313

Angler's Workshop
P.O. Box 1044
Woodland, WA 98674
(360) 225-9445

Dan Bailey's Fly Shop
P.O. Box 1019
Livingston, MT 59047
(800) 356-4052

Barlow's Tackle Shop
Box 830369
Richardson, TX 75080
(214) 231-5982

L.L. Bean, Inc.
Freeport, ME 04033
(800) 221-4221

Blue Ridge Rod Company
P.O. Box 6268
Annapolis, MD 21401
(410) 224-4072

Cabela's
812 13th Avenue
Sidney, NE 69160
(800) 237-4444

Captain Harry's Fishing Supply
100 NE 11th Street
Miami, FL 33132
(800) 327-4088

Cold Spring Anglers
P.O. Box 129
Carlisle, PA 17013
(800) 248-8937

Feather-Craft Fly Fishing
8307 Manchester Road
P.O. Box 19904
St. Louis, MO 63144
(800) 659-1707

Fishing Creek Outfitters
RR 1, Box 310-1
Benton, PA 17814
(800) 548-0093

Flyfisher's Paradise
2603 East College Avenue
State College, PA 16801
(814) 234-4189

The Fly Shop
4140 Churn Creek Road
Redding, CA 96002
(800) 669-FISH

Frontier Anglers
P.O. Box 11
Dilon, MT 59725
(800) 228-5263

Gander Mountain
P.O. Box 248
Wilmot, WI 53192
(800) 558-9410

The Global Flyfisher
2849 West Dundee Road
Suite 132
Northbrook, IL 60062
(800) 457-7026

Gorilla and Sons
Box 2309
Bellingham, WA 98227
(800) 246-7455

Henrickson Rod Company
3825 Hollow Creek
Fortworth, TX 76116
(800) 933-7637

Henry's Fork Anglers
HC 66, Box 491
Island Park, ID 83429
(208) 558-7525

The Hook & Hackle Company
7 Kaycee Loop Road
Plattsburg, NY 12901
(518) 561-5893

Hunters Angling Supplies
1 Central Square
New Boston, NH 03070
(800) 331-8558

International Angler
503 Freeport Road
Pittsburg, PA 15215
(800) 782-4222

Jann's Sportman's Supplies
P.O. Box 89
Maumee, OH 43537
(800) 346-6590

K & K Flyfisher's Supply
8643 Grant
Overlook Park, KS 66212
(800) 795-8118

Kettle Creek Tackle Shop
HCR 62, Box 140
Renovo, PA 17754
(717) 923-1416

Madison River Fishing Company
109 Main Street
P.O. Box 627
Ennis, MT 59729
(800) 227-7127

Marriott's Fly Fishing
2700 West Orangethorpe
Fullerton, CA 92633
(800) 367-2299 (California)
(800) 535-6633 (elsewhere)

Murray's Fly Shop
P.O. Box 156
Edinburg, VA 22824
(540) 984-4212

Muskie Fever
P.O. Box 32011
Minneapolis, MN 55432
(800) 458-1205

On The Fly
3628 Sage Drive
Rockford, IL 61114
(815) 877-0090

Orvis
1711 Blue Hills Drive
Roanoke, VA 24022
(800) 541-3541

Pennsylvania Outdoor Warehouse
1508 Memorial Avenue
Williamsport, PA 17701
(800) 441-7685

Fred Reese's Trout Shop
220 Thompson Street
Jersey Shore, PA 17740
(717) 398-3016

The Surfcaster
P.O. Box 1731
Darien, CT 06820
(800) 551-SURF

Swallow's Nest
2308 6th Avenue
Seattle, WA 98121
(800) 676-4041

Terminal Tackle Co.
P.O. Box 427
Kings Park, NY 11754
(516) 269-6005

Urban Angler Ltd.
118 East 25th Street
3rd floor
New York, NY 10010
(212) 979-7600

Westbank Anglers
P.O. Box 523
Teton Village, WY 83025
(800) 922-3474

Organizations and Associations

American Littoral Society
Building 18
Sandy Hook
Highlands, NJ 07732
(908) 291-0055

Atlantic Salmon Federation
P.O. Box 429
St. Andrews, New Brunswick
EOG 2X0 Canada
(506) 529-4581

Bass Angler's Sportsman Society
(B.A.S.S.)
5845 Carmichael Road
Montgomery, AL 36117
(205) 272-9530

Bass'n Gal
P.O. Box 13925
Arlington, TX 76013
(817) 265-6214

British Field Sports Association
59 Kennington Road
London SEI 7PZ, England
071-928-4742

Federation of Fly Fishers
P.O. Box 1595
Bozeman, MT 59771
(406) 585-7592

Fish Unlimited
P.O. Box 1073
Shelter Island Heights, NY 11965
(516) 749-FISH

Future Fisherman Foundation
1033 N. Fairfax Street
Suite 200
Alexandria, VA 22314
(703) 519-9691

International Game Fish Association
1301 East Atlantic Blvd.
Pompano Beach, FL 33060
(305) 941-3474

Izaak Walton League of America
1401 Wilson Blvd.
Level B
Arlington, VA 22209
(703) 528-1818

Outdoor Writers Association
of America
2017 Cato Avenue
Suite 101
State College, PA 16801
(814) 234-1011

Salmon and Trout Association
Fishmongers Hall
London Bridge
London SEI 7PZ
England
071-283-5838

Theodore Gordon Flyfishers
24 East 39 Street
New York, NY 10156
(212) 689-1155

Trout Unlimited
501 Church Street
Vienna, VA 22180
(703) 281-1100
(800) 834-2491

Pic's Pogy by Tom Piccolo.

Uni-Knot

Use to tie fly to tippet. Creates a sliding loop that can be left open or tightened against hook eye. This loop lets nymphs and other subsurface flies "swim" in the water and bass bugs pop better.

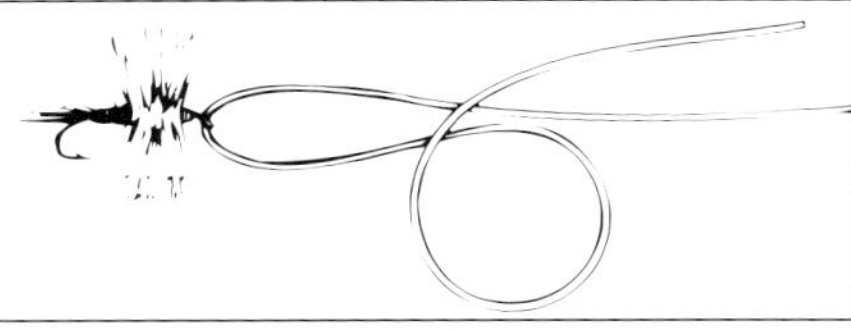

Pass 6" to 8" of the tag end of tippet through the eye of hook. Form a 1 ½" diameter loop with tag end.

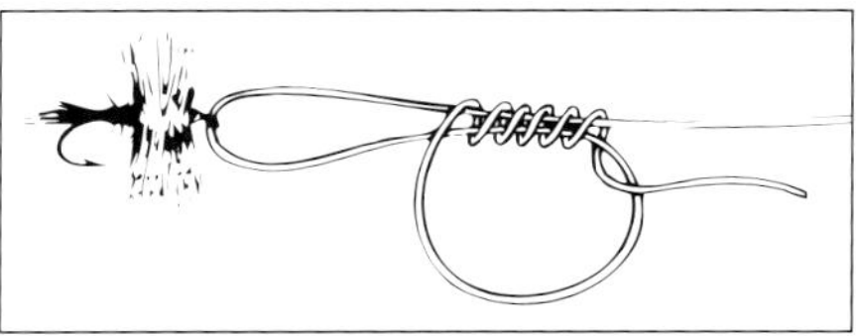

Pass tag through and around loop and tippet five times, moving away from the fly.

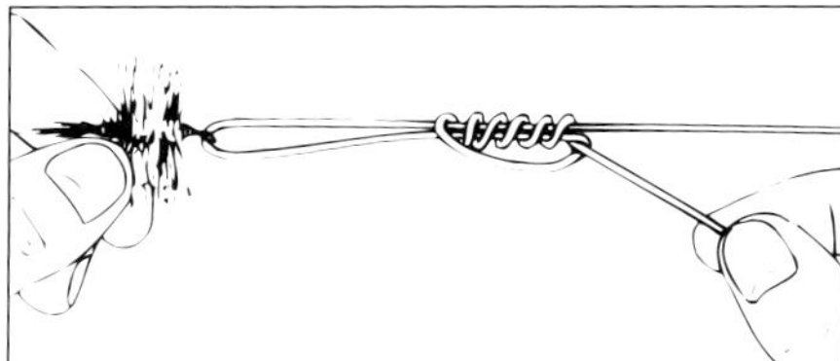

Lubricate, and tighten knot by pulling very tightly on tag end. The degree of tightening determines how the knot slides on tippet for keeping loop open or sliding it closed. With heavy tippet material (over .011"), grasp the tag end with pliers or hemostats and tighten the knot.

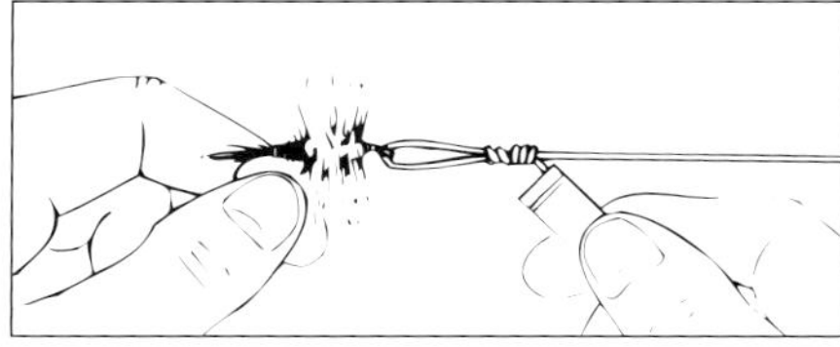

Adjust loop between fly and knot as desired. Trim tag end.

Blood Knot

Use to tie tippet to end of leader or join sections of tapered leaders.

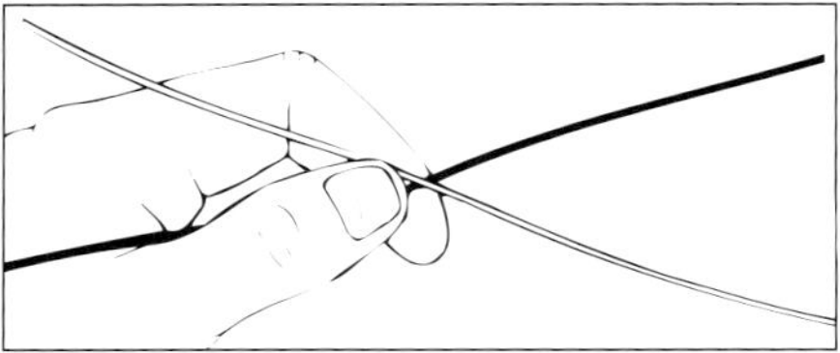

Cross both pieces of material in an "X", leaving at least 8" of overlap.

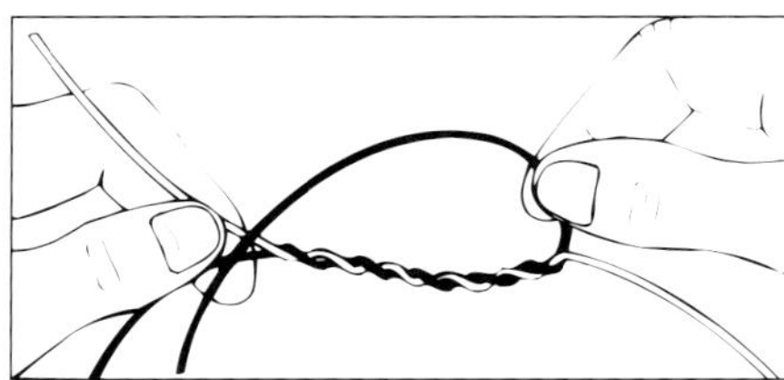

Wind one end around the standing part of the other piece five times and pass the end of the other side of the "X" formed by the intersection of the two pieces.

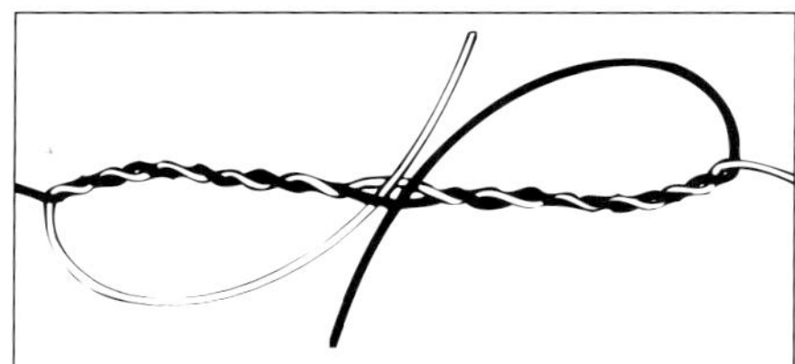

Pinch the line at this point and with the other hand wind the free end around the standing piece in the opposite direction five times. Pass this end through the same loop as the first end, but go through the loop in the opposite direction.

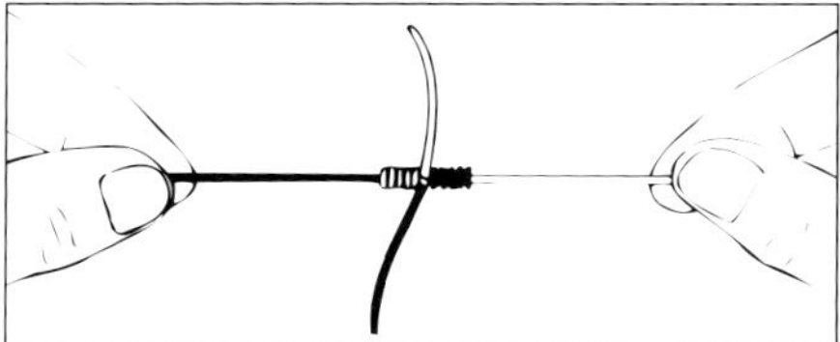

Lubricate and hold both ends together while pulling on the standing parts to tighten. The easiest way to keep the ends from slipping through is to hold them in your teeth. Don't put any pressure on the short ends while tightening. Trim tag ends as close to the knot as possible.

Surgeon's Loop

Use to tie the loop in the end of the leader.

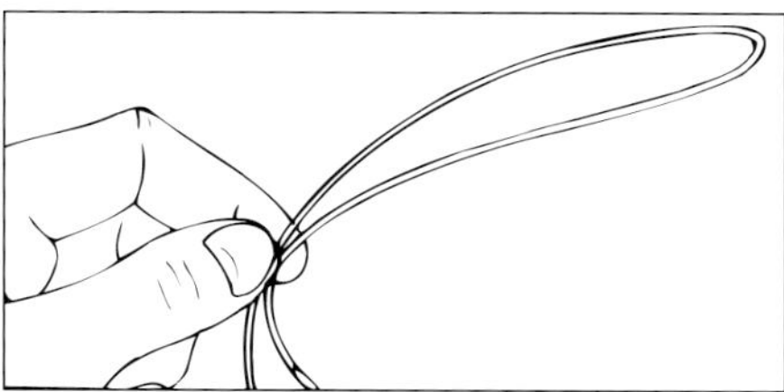

Form a loop in the end of the leader.

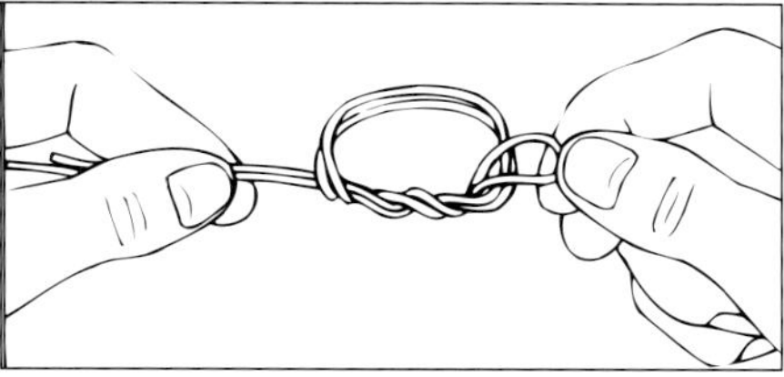

Make a simple overhand knot in the double line.

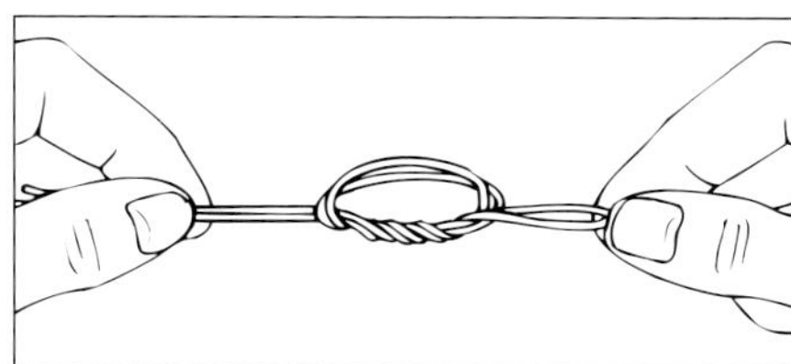

Then bring the loop end through the overhand knot again. Lubricate, and tighten by pulling on the loop end with one hand and the standing leader and tag end in the other.

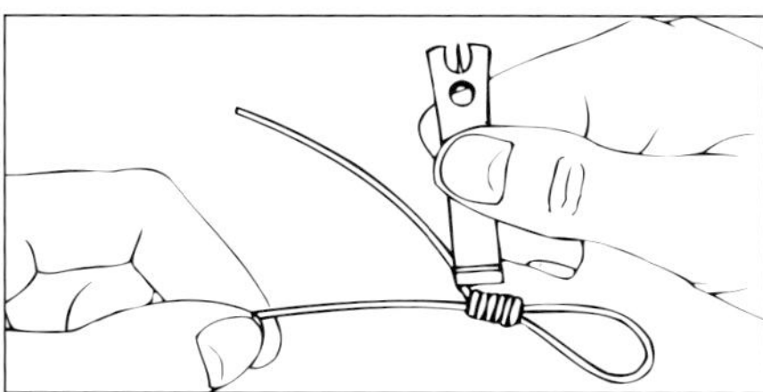

Trim.

Clinch Knot

Use to tie fly to end of tippet. Sometimes tied as an "improved" clinch knot by passing the tag end back through the loop created at the end of step three.

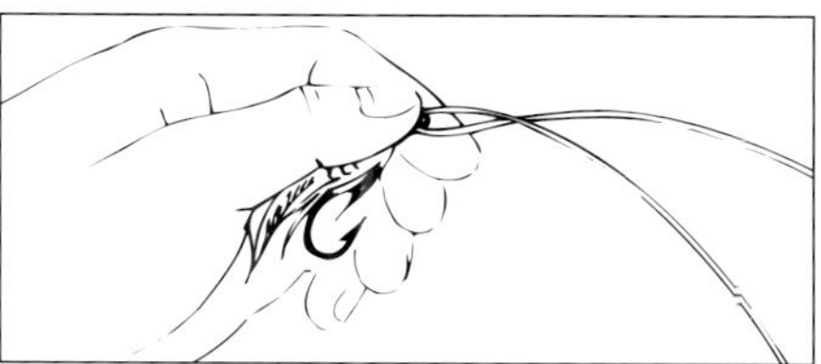

Insert 6" to 8" of tippet through eye of hook.

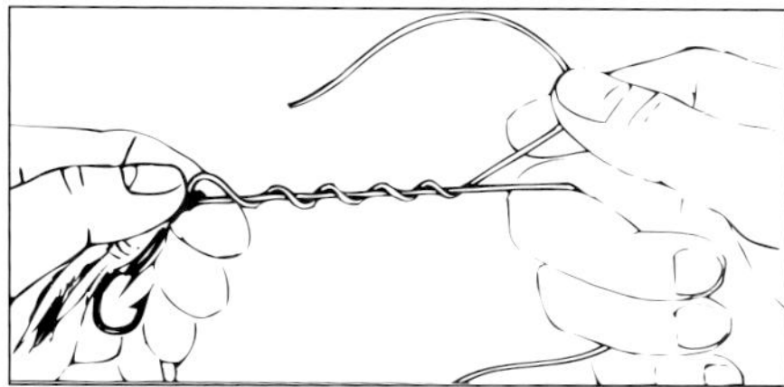

Hold fly in left hand and with right hand wind the end of the leader around the standing part of the leader five times, keeping a small loop open immediately adjacent to hook eye, pinched between thumb and forefinger.

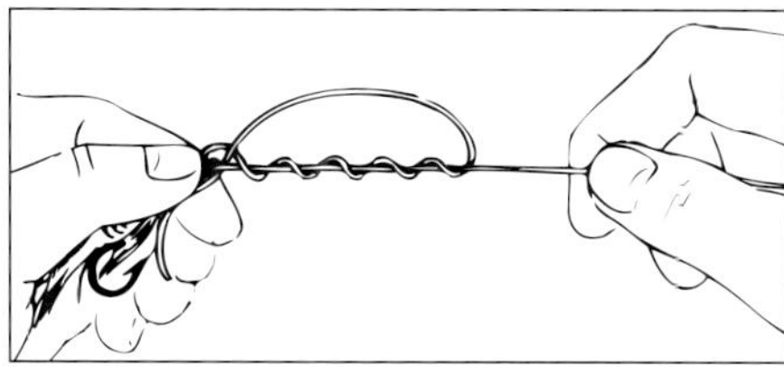

Bring tag end of leader through loop next to the hook eye and grasp with thumb and forefinger.

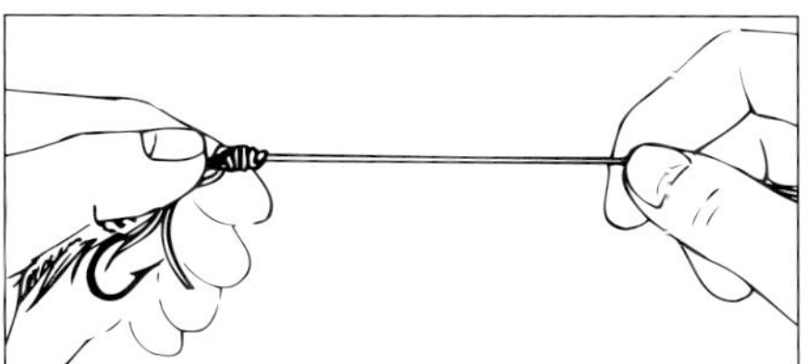

Lubricate, and tighten by pulling the standing part of the leader and the fly in opposite directions. Do not pull on the tag end of the leader— hold it alongside the fly. Trim tag end close to knot.

Materials List

Northeast

Brettell Mackerel Streamer

BODY: Black and green neck (stiff).
HEAD: Red thread and cement.
HOOK: Eagle claw 2/0 S.S. Popper hooks.

Chartreuse Fish Head

COLOR: Olive on top, orange or olive lateral line.
EYES: Black on yellow.
FISHHEAD: 1/2" or 1/3" gold or 1/3" White Corsair tubing.
HOOK: M34007 or 34011, No. 1/0.
SIDEFLASH: Pearl or olive Flashabou.
SKIRT: Chartreuse marabou, white marabou.
TAILWING: Chartreuse saddle or neck feathers.
THREAD: 6/0, Danville.

Johnny's Anchovy

BODY: Rusty brown Super Hair, pearl Flashabou, white Super Hair, silicone.
EYES: Stick-on Prismatic.
HOOK: Eagle Claw 254 SS size 1.

Martha's Vineyard Squid

BODY: Krystal chenille, glimmer, G.E. silicone 2, large stick-on eyes.
HOOK: Mustad 3411 3/0 hook.
TAIL: Saddle hackles.

Mullet

BODY: Silvery blue den marabou feather, pink and olive marabou feather, olive saddle hackles, badger hackles, silver pheasant feathers, white deer body hair.
HEAD: 1/4" glass eyes, wire, deer body hair.
UNDERBODY: White marabou feather.

Pic-a-bugger

BODY: Chartreuse saddle hackle, holographic fly fiber, medium chartreuse chenille.
COLLAR: Wide chartreuse saddle hackle.
HEAD: Chartreuse tying thread with red band.
HOOK: Mustad 34007, Daiichi 2546, Partridge "Sea Prince" size 2 and 1/0.
TAIL: Chartreuse marabou, Krystal Flash.
THREAD: Chartreuse, Danville Flat Wax Nylon or Danville Plus.

Sea Wulff

BODY: Grizzly hackle, colored Fish Hair.
HEAD: 20-lb. test plastic-coated braided wire, embedded.
HOOK: 1/0 Eagle Claw, No. 254N.

Snake Fly

HEAD: Deer body hair.
HOOK: Straight eye, standard length No. 4 to 2/0.
TAIL: Ostrich herl.
WINGS: Marabou.

Mid-Atlantic

AlbaClouser

HEAD: Medium (7/32) lead eyes

painted silver with black pupil.
HOOK: No. 2 mustad 34007 or Tiemco 811S.
MIDDLE WING: White or clear Ultra Hair, silver Krystal Flash.
TAIL/BODY: White or clear Ultra Hair or Super Hair.
THREAD: Clear monofilament.
TOP WING: Light olive, smoke, or chartreuse Ultra Hair or Super Hair.

Bionic Butterfish

BODY: Silver poly flash, pearl and silver Firefly Tie, silver Flashabou.
COLLAR: White bucktail, silver Firefly Tie.
EYES: Large prismatic stick-on eyes.
GILLS: Red marabou.
HOOKS: 3/0 and 5/0 heavy gauge stainless in tandem.
TAIL: White saddle hackles.
THREAD: Size A white nylon.
WINGS: White saddles.

Clouser Deep Minnow

CENTER LINE: Krystal Flash or Flashabou.
EYES: Metallic eyes 4/32 to 7/32 diameter.
HEAD: Thread 6/0, 3/0, flymaster plus.
HOOK: Mustad 3906B or TMC 3761 sizes 2-4-6; Salt Water Mustad 34007 or TMC 811S sizes 3/0 to 8.
WINGS/BACK/BELLY: Deer tail hair, Ultra Hair, Super Hair, calf tail, animal guard hairs, and other suitable materials.

D.L.'s Mylar Needlefish

BODY: Clear fine monofilament thread, fine mylar tubing (overbody), Pearlescent, Fine Mylar Tubing (underbody), Ultra fine green glitter, 5-minute epoxy
HEAD: No. 2 witchcraft eyes, green permanent marking pencil.
HOOK: 34007 No. 2.
TAIL: Black hackle.

Lefty's Deceiver

COLLAR: White bucktail.
HEAD: Green thread.
HOOK: No. 6, 3/0 straight eye standard length hook mylar.
THROAT: Red Flashabou.
TOPPING: Peacock herl.
WINGS: White saddle hackles with grizzly, pearl mylar, Krystal Flash or Flashabou.

Mega Mackerel

BODY: Silver polyflash, blue and lime firefly tie, silver Flashabou.
COLLAR: White bucktail, chartreuse and blue bucktail, blue and lime firefly tie.
EYES: Large prismatic stick-on eyes.
GILLS: Red marabou.
HOOKS: 3/0 & 5/0 heavy gauge stainless in tandem.
TAIL: White saddle hackles.
THREAD: Size A white nylon.
WINGS: Dyed blue, chartreuse and natural grizzly saddles, white saddles.

The Pops

BODY: Orvis rattle, fly foam, Flexo, witchcraft eyes, Aqua seal, Berol Prismacolor marker.
HEAD: Mono thread.
HOOK: Mustad 90233S or Tiemco 5110 2/0, 1/0, 2, 6.

TAIL: Hen saddle hackle, Krystal Flash, saddle palmer.

Shine Tail

BODY: Bugskin inserted into tubing.
HEAD: Stick on eyes, permanent marking pencil.
HOOK: No. 1 to 2/0 hooks.
TAIL: Bugskin.
OTHER: Epoxy, 1/4", 1/8", 1/3" Corsair tubing.

Florida Keys

Bonefish Special

BODY: Gold mylar, gold monofilament (20-, 25-, or 30-lb. test, depending on weight and bulk desired).
HOOK: No. 4, Mustad 34007.
TAIL: Black thread, orange marabou or pin feather of saddle.
WINGS: Preferably bucktail; otherwise calftail or fish hair.

Buchanan Special

COLLAR: Chocolate brown saddle hackle.
HEAD: Fluorescent orange thread.
HOOK: Eagle claw LO545S 2/0.
TAIL: Orange Krystal Flash, grizzly dyed tangerine hackle tips.

Chernobyl Crab

BODY: Grizzly hackle, badger hackle, deer body hair.
HOOK: Teimco 811S or mustad 34007 No. 2, 2/0.
TAIL: Krystal Flash, calf tail.

Flats Master

BODY: Danville's flat waxed thread (colors: pink, orange, white, fluorescent chartreuse, or yellow).
HEAD: Bead chain (eyes), Grizzly hackle (collar).
HOOK: Mustad 34007 No. 2 thru No. 6.
OVERWING: Tan Craft Fur.
TAIL: Marabou (color to match body), pearlescent Krystal Flash.

Hot Lips

BODY: Sheet foam.
EYES: Magic marker.
HOOK: 34007-2/0 mustad.
TAIL: Chicken feathers and Krystal Flash, palmer of marabou.
THROAT: Ice chenille.

Marquesa Sunrise Special

BODY: Palmered grizzly hackle, orange grizzly.
HEAD: Orange thread, clear epoxy.
HOOK: Eagle claw D067.
TAIL: Gold Flashabou or Krystal Flash.
OTHER: Tan marabou.

Gulf of Mexico

Brooks's Shrimp

BODY: Creamy white Seal-ex.
CARAPACE: White swiss straw.
EYES: Mono nymph eyes.
FEELERS: Grizzly cock hackle.
HOOK: 34011, number 2 to 4.
LEGS: Pearl crystal chenille (long fiber).
ROSTRUM: Bleached short deer body hair.

TENTACLES: Black horse mane or Ultra Hair.
THREAD: White 3/0.
UNDER WING: White or cream marabou.
WEED GUARD: Hard mason 15, 20, 25 lb., depending on hook size.

Caribou Shrimp

ANTENNAE/ROSTRUM/FEELERS: Tips of caribou body hair.
BODY: Spun caribou, trimmed flat on top and bottom.
EYES: Umpqua mono nymph eyes.
HOOK: No. 4, Mustad 34007.
LEGS: Badger saddle hackle palmered through body and trimmed on top.
THREAD: White 3/0.

Crustacean A.D.

ANTENNAE: 30-lb. extra stiff black monofilament.
BODY: Extra small chenille, size 00.
CEMENT: Thinned pliobond, thinned goop or flexament, thinned head cement, head cement, and super glue.
EYES: Monofilament, 50-lb. test, 1 1/2 inches long.
HACKLE: Extra long saddle hackle 4 1/2 to 5 inches long after webby part is removed.
HOOK: Mustad No. 34011, size 2.
OVERBODY: Glimmer flash chenille.
RIBBING: White, nylon thread size 2/0 or 3/0.
SHELL: 3/16 inch diameter pearlescent tubing.
TAIL: Fox squirrel tail or fish hair and Flashabou.
THREAD: 2/0 flat nylon or 3/0 waxed monocord.
WEIGHT: Round lead wire 1/16 inch in diameter.

Glass Minnow

BODY: Buck tail, aluminum foil, monofilament.
HEAD: Red or black thread.
HOOK: No. 2 or No. 4 O'Shaughnessy hook-3407 Mustad or 9255PS VMC.
TAIL: Buck tail.
OTHER: Wrap on a head and whip finish, head cement.

Kirk's Rattle Rouser

BODY: Extra-large mylar tubing, with a BB and a plastic Woodie's Rattle inside, epoxy.
EYES: Acrylic paint.
HOOK: Mustad 34011, size 6 to 2/0; just about any long-shank, ring-eye hook will work.
TAIL: Teased-out mylar tubing.
THREAD: Danville Flymaster Plus, orange or red thread.
WING: Bucktail and Krystal Flash or Flashabou.

Snook-a-roo

COLLAR: Pointed white deer body hair.
EYES: 9mm blue solid plastic doll or cat eyes.
HEAD/BODY: White deer hair with a stacked black spot on top, inside a stacked nat grey spot.
HOOK: Straight eye, standard length (VMC 2/0).
SKIRT: Red stripped and folded marabou.
TAIL: White bucktail, white grizzly large neck hackles, silver straws of Flashabou, chartreuse Krystal Flash.

Big Game Key Lime Squid

BODY: Tube 1/8" O.D. NyLaflo High Pressure tubing; 1/8" I.D. PVC tubing glued to hard tubing, white thread.
HEAD: 5 minute epoxy, 15mm oval doll eyes, black on white; plastic black on amber (eyes).
HOOK: Not rigged; tandem tube flies.
TAIL: Chartreuse top, white bottom, chartreuse witchcraft tape.
OTHER: Chartreuse foam head.

Billfish Fly

BODY: Fish Hair.
HEAD: Heavy thread and clear epoxy, Shock Tippet is run through the tube in the head.
HOOK: Stinger hook 4/0 and 6/0, dental tape (not floss), silver mylar.
OTHER: Foam popper head.
COLOR VARIATIONS: blue/white, blue/green/white, green/yellow, all white, and orange/yellow.

Johnson Sand Lance

HEAD: Epoxy, witchcraft eyes.
HOOK: Partridge Sea Prince (size 2 to 8, depending upon size of fly).
LATERAL LINE: Narrow olive holographic mylar tinsel, olive Super Hair.
THREAD: Clear monofilament.
TUBE: Plastic Slipstream (Veniards, UK), or Kennebec Fly & Tackle tubes (Yarmouth, ME).
WINGS: Olive Super Hair, pink Super Hair, white Super Hair; silver diamond braid.

Krystal Flash

EYES: Black pupil over yellow paint.
HEAD: Thread over Krystal Flash, epoxy or head cement.
HOOK: 34007, 34011 2-4/0.
THREAD: Transparent sewing thread.
WING: Underwing White Bucktail in the round, Overwing Pearl Krystal Flash in the round, peacock on top.
VARIATIONS: Krystal Flash wing may be blue, green, pink, black, or pearl.

Del's Permit Fly

BODY: Hackle tips, bright chartreuse thread.
HEAD: Lead chrome eyes.
HOOK: No. 1 to 2/0 straight eye standard length hook 34007.
TAIL: Pearl Flashabou.
OTHER: Rubber bands, tan and brown red-tipped acrylic yarn.

Pete's Slider

BODY: Dynacord 3/0 or Kevlar, any color thread, 1/2" Poly Foam Caulk Saver, foam cylinder, 1/2" mylar "Pearl" tubing, red cactus Chenile or Estaz.
HEAD: Hot glue dipped in glitter, marker pens, decal 6mm (eyes), red marker pen (gills).
HOOK: Eagle Claw 66S 4/0.
FINISH: Soft Body Epoxy.
TAIL: White bucktail, olive Super Hair, peacock flash.

Whistler

BODY: Medium red chenille.
FLASHTAIL: Silver Flashabou, bucktail.

HACKLE COLLAR: Webby saddle hackles.
HEAD: Silver bead chain eyes, red tying thread.
HOOK: Straight eye standard length No. 2 to 3/0.
SHOULDER: Grizzly neck hackle.
SIDEFLASH: Multi-colored Krystal Flash, length of bucktail.
TAIL/WING: White bucktail.
UNDER BODY: Lead wire (.030).

United Kingdom

Clan Chief

BODY: Black seal's fur/ substitute.
BODY HACKLES: Scarlet and black cock hackles.
HEAD HACKLE: Black hen.
RIB: Medium oval silver.
TAG: Two turns of flat silver tinsel.
TAIL: Two parts–scarlet wool above, yellow wool below.

Kildonan Killer

BODY: Black seal's fur teased out.
HEAD HACKLE: Ilen blue peacock neck feather with short blue hackle.
RIB: Oval silver.
TAG: Silver tinsel.
TAIL: Jungle cock.

Euro Shrimp

BODY CASE: Plastic drinking straw (hinged section).
EYES: Dressmakers pins (black).
HEAD/FEELERS: Heron or pheasant rump feather fibers mixed with synthetics, i.e., organser or crimped nylon (Ultra Hair).
HOOK: Size 1/0 to 4/0, English Bait Hook (or similar shape).
UNDER BODY: Wool or sparkle (type) chenille, palmered heron or pheasant rump feather.
OTHER: Permanent marker pen, light coating of epoxy resin.

Denmark

Sideliner

BODY: White SLF dubbing, black antron.
EYES: Bead.
HACKLE: Orange soft fibers (Hoffmann Softhackle).
HEAD: Black.
HOOK: Partridge GRS CS 11, size 4 to 10.
RIB: Goldwire.
WINGS: Rabbit strip olive.

Acknowledgments

A great debt is owed to all the fly tiers and designers contained in this volume, for all their time and energies spent helping me understand the details of their craft.

I am indebted to the American Museum of Fly Fishing for use of their collection of flies and fly fishing paraphernalia—especially Jon Mathewson, Craig Gilborn, and the rest of the crew. The A.M.F.F., a nonprofit, educational institution dedicated to preserving the rich heritage of fly fishing, serves as a repository for, and conservator to, the world's largest collection of angling-related objects. For further information contact: The American Museum of Fly Fishing, P.O. Box 42, Manchester, VT 05254, (802)362-3300.

Many thanks also to The Orvis Company, Inc., especially Paul Ferson and Tom Rosenbauer, for the use of a selection of their equipment and supplies, for much help in creating my roster of saltwater tiers, and for the information and illustrations contained herein from The Orvis Knot Booklet. For information contact: The Orvis Company, Inc., Historic Route 7A, Manchester, VT 05254, (800)548-9548.

For their assistance in establishing contacts with charter boat captains, lodging, designers, etc., thanks to Bay Street Outfitters in Beaufort, SC and Barnes Outfitters in Portland, ME; the Vermont Travel and Tourism Board; the South Carolina Department of Travel and Tourism; the North Carolina Travel and Tourism; the North Carolina Wildlife Resources Commission; the South Carolina Wildlife and Marine Resources Department; Maine Office of Tourism; Nancy Marshall Communications; and the Manchester, VT, Chamber of Commerce. For lodging and logistic support, thanks to the wonderful Equinox Hotel and the Brittany Inn of Manchester, VT; the exquisite Hyatt Grand Cypress and Walt Disney World Dolphin Hotel in Orlando, FL; Sugarloaf/USA; the Phenix Inn of Bangor, ME; and the Holiday Inn by the Bay of Portland, ME.

Thanks to everyone at Balliett & Fitzgerald, including Duncan Bock and Howard Slatkin, editors; Chris Mitchell, copy editor; Ruth Ro, Donna Spillane, and Cate O'Brien, editorial assistants; and special thanks to Maria Fernandez, photo editor.

Thanks to my editor at Bulfinch Press, Dorothy Williams. I am also grateful to Nikon Professional Services for their technical assistance, and Fuji Film for great new films. Many thanks to my grandfather and father who originally lured me into the sport and finally, to my wife Judith, who would allow me many more hours fishing than I can actually find.

HARDY